I DON'T WANT TO DIE POOR

DISCARD

ALSO BY MICHAEL ARCENEAUX

I Can't Date Jesus

I DON'T WANT TO DIE POOR

ESSAYS

MICHAEL ARCENEAUX

ATRIA PAPERBACK

NEW YORK   LONDON   TORONTO   SYDNEY   NEW DELHI

ATRIA
PAPERBACK

An Imprint of Simon & Schuster, Inc.
1230 Avenue of the Americas
New York, NY 10020

First Atria Paperback edition April 2020

ATRIA PAPERBACK and colophon are trademarks of
Simon & Schuster, Inc.

For information about special discounts for bulk purchases,
please contact Simon & Schuster Special Sales at 1-866-506-1949
or business@simonandschuster.com.

The Simon & Schuster Speakers Bureau can bring authors to
your live event. For more information or to book an event, contact
the Simon & Schuster Speakers Bureau at 1-866-248-3049 or
visit our website at www.simonspeakers.com.

Interior design by Erika Genova

Manufactured in the United States of America

1   3   5   7   9   10   8   6   4   2

Library of Congress Cataloging-in-Publication Data has been applied for.

ISBN 978-1-9821-2930-9
ISBN 978-1-9821-2931-6 (ebook)

To every single customer service rep employed by Discover Student Loans or Navient, this book is not dedicated to you, but I would like to extend a fuck you to each of you for disturbing me with your calls while I was writing this book.

Had you given me a little peace, you would've gotten your money sooner.

With that out of the way, this book is dedicated to my mama. Thank you for making my life so.

It's expensive to be me.
—*Erika Jayne*

Throw that money over here, nigga,
that's what it's for.
—*Cardi B*

Contents

I DON'T WANT TO DIE POOR

YOU SELF-CENTERED BASTARD

Of course it was an attractive light-skinned Black man who led me to ruin.

Men are generally awful, but there is something unique about this particular genre of bae. I can't recall his name, but when your face looks like the reason God created sin, does it matter?

I will never forget spotting him in the cafeteria and immediately wanting to venture over his way to listen to whatever it was he had to say. I may have been unwilling at the time to admit the truth about my same-sex attractions out loud, but when temptation is mere feet in front of you with a smile and overall profile that gives "leading man in a 1990s Black romantic comedy" or at least an ill-advised reboot of one, you shimmy your gay ass over and try not to stare too hard.

We were both at James Madison Senior High School's College Fair, which for all intents and purposes, I, as a student at James Madison Senior High School, was not especially excited about attending. He appeared younger than his recruiting counterparts around us—had to have been in his mid to late twenties. God, I wish Instagram had been around in 2001, so that I had photographic evidence of how he looked.

Back then, I used to describe Madison as the local version of *Lean on Me*, only our Joe Clark liked to wear cowboy boots and somehow came across even surlier and stricter than the "Crazy Joe" at (Fair) Eastside High that Morgan Freeman played. I remember once showing someone I was communicating with through a message board a picture of my high school.

"Nigga, that looks like a prison!"

Or if one were to be a bit more generous as a result of high school pride, perhaps it resembled a juvenile detention center whose best days may indeed have been well behind it, but at least the people in charge had gone out and bought some paint to try and spruce the place up. (As much sprucing as you could do to an older building surrounded by fencing and large gates.) The original building has since been demolished and a new structure has opened in its place. I drove by it during a work-related trip back to my hometown of Houston, Texas. It now looks like a much fancier private prison, although whoever picked the colors for it does not watch enough Bravo or HGTV.

In a lot of ways, I felt as if we students were treated like prisoners. We had a magnet program for meteorology, which, with all due respect to Al Roker, icon, never made sense to me given that, at an "inner city high school" there weren't many Black and Latinx teens who thought they could one day tell viewers that Captain Planet was correct and Mother Nature's revenge was imminent. I was not in the magnet program, but I did take mostly pre-AP courses, and as a result of that, I did have some teachers who pushed me a little harder as a student. Even so, the overall climate of the school felt far stricter than it needed to be, in an effort to corral the "unruly" minority population of largely meager means, who most outsiders assumed had very little to hope for when it came to their futures.

My high school made national headlines in spring 2019 when the principal announced a dress code for parents that many rightly regarded as classist. To any Madison alum of a certain age group, the news was unsettling but not at all surprising. I remember the principal who took the place of Joe Clark's Cowboy Cousin (after his promotion) attempting to ban the class ahead of mine from wearing braids and locs at commencement. That was ultimately overturned because of pushback from students, but respectability was, as usual, pushed by the repressive.

No matter, though: I'm a proud Marlin. I can be critical because I went there and understand. I can recognize that in the midst of all that, there were good teachers, there were bright minds, and there were plenty of us with loads of potential. More of us just needed convincing of what could be possible, along with access and means to arrive there.

As for the college fair, the obvious colleges were present: the HBCUs Texas Southern University and Prairie View A&M University. Obvious is not used pejoratively. Some of the most brilliant people I have ever met in my life attended or have taught at either school, but in terms of the collective expectations of the student body, they were considered our main, and limited, options.

To be fair, so were some of the other Texas-based schools that seemed to want to court at least two and a half of us to help offset their lily-white campuses. Say, the University of Houston, the University of Texas at Austin, Texas A&M University, and Sam Houston State University. There were people who worked at all these schools actively pushing us to entertain the idea of venturing out, but the army recruiters were getting a big share of the attention all the same.

The very handsome college recruiter I was entranced by was representing Hampton University, a school I had never heard of but had appreciation for based on their blue-and-white aesthetic and choice in spokespeople.

While it was a forgone conclusion at this point that I would be attending college, in hindsight, it was far more of an anomaly for me than I knew at the time. My mom had effectively drilled it into me for as long as I remembered that I was going to college, but this wasn't really the norm for those that grew up around me or shared my bloodline. Still, I knew my ass was going because I was not going to have that woman choke me out with a rosary until I acted like I had some damn sense.

I dreamed of New York University or Columbia University, but who had money for that? My mother made clear that I would go somewhere, but neither she nor I had entertained the idea that I might attend the kind of school that felt like an unattainable fantasy. My assumption was that I was likely to go to University of Houston, though if I lucked up, maybe I could get scholarship money out of UT Austin and go there instead.

After talking to Recruiter Bae, my feelings changed. He convinced me that if I wanted to attend a prestigious college— private, out of state, even—it was possible, no matter what my surroundings or financial circumstances suggested. When he asked what I wanted to do with my life and I mentioned journalism and television, he boasted about Hampton and some of its alum. While I make no apologies for letting hormones steer me in his direction, he was genuinely inspiring to me, and while some of the schools I've attended were met with jeers from others who were from Houston but came from much nicer backgrounds, it's often been in those settings that someone Black has looked me square in the eye and instilled in me the belief that what seems unattainable is entirely possible.

I recall his fine ass inspiring a lot of others, too. So much so that he became the focus of conversation in some AP class. I remember one of my classmates specifically saying, "All of y'all talking about going to Hampton or whatever are going to be right here with me at TSU or PV." Not long before the declaration, I recall her wanting to go to Florida A&M University. Not sure what changed her mind—presumably the cost of the school—but her swatting away one of her goals under the pretense of realism had spurred in her the self-appointed task of doing the same to the rest of us. She ended up being correct about where most ended up, but I took what Recruiter Bae had to say to heart and tried to make a miracle happen.

It was the first semester of my senior year, so there wasn't a lot of time to figure a lot of this out. I did apply to several schools out of state and ended up deciding to attend Howard University in Washington, D.C. For me, once I got to see the kind of people who'd gone there—including Houston natives Debbie Allen and Phylicia Rashad—it felt like the best place for me to be. Best because it felt not only the most reasonable choice, but the most viable. I knew someone who had grown up around the corner from me and had gone to one of those fancy New York schools, and who left a year after because of the enormous tuition bill. (He married rich; he's fine.) I didn't want that to happen to me, and to be honest, I couldn't even afford these well-to-do Black-ass schools, so why in the hell was I going to try to go to one of those?

To try and pay for Howard, I applied to as many scholarships as I could find. I wound up winning seventeen in a single semester. I have thought a lot about what my life would have been like if someone had convinced me that I could leave the state of Texas for college sooner. I could have amassed a lot more in scholarship money if I had been convinced a year prior to allow myself to dream a bit bigger. I have also thought a lot about what my life would have been like if I had even accepted being gay before I left for college.

I won one of my closest friends a $10,000 scholarship by writing her essay. I know this because they told her that her remarkably well-written entry was what won them over. That should have been me! But because I had a thing for suppression and stubbornness, I did not pursue queer-centered scholarships and wound up turning to Citibank to cover the rest.

My mama was never into this idea. In fact, I remember once being excited about an acceptance letter from another school and watching her burst into rage. She was in the kitchen while I excitedly shared the news. Then she just got quiet. Finally, she slammed the kitchen cabinet and let out what she had appeared to be holding in for quite some time.

You self-centered bastard.

She didn't apologize for that comment until about two years after that, when I brought it up in conversation in the car, but even if hearing my own mom say such a thing to me stung, I did try to consider the source of her anger. We didn't have the money for any of these schools I was considering. Who was I to know this and pursue them so vehemently anyway? How did I not consider how that might impact others around me— namely her? I didn't think I was being selfish, but I understand now why I came across that way.

I didn't want to be stuck in Houston. I didn't want to delay my dreams, because I worried that if I did, they might never come true. I felt like I was raised by two people who had had their dreams stripped from them. I grew up around people who didn't appear to have ever even had the chance to dream. I was Black, from Hiram Clarke, and didn't know any damn body with even a molecule of the level of access needed to have some sustainable career in media and television.

I dreamed for it anyway, and much of the gumption to do so was rooted in my mom's encouragement—no matter our disagreement on how to go about it. Even if she disagreed with me, she supported me, and that says everything about her. But what was never said between us in those moments was another truth about why I was so desperate to get out: I didn't want to be stuck in a violent home that made me want to die, more than I ever admitted to anyone else in that house. I needed to get out for not only my dreams, but my sanity. Howard University felt like my best bet to do both.

I took out about $10,000 in loans for the first year, but it soon became clear that I'd need much more to keep studying at Howard and living in Washington until graduation. So I took out more. I struggled a lot in college and ended up losing a few of those scholarships. Midway through my time at Howard, I decided that it might be in my best interest to go back home and figure out another plan. Part of that plan included me transferring to the University of Houston.

I got accepted and planned to start my junior year there; however, one trip back home during Spring Break of my sophomore year showed me that while I wasn't my happiest yet at Howard, I for damn sure wouldn't be happy back in Houston. My dad was drunk, argumentative, and ultimately, violent. By now I was on the verge of turning twenty, and sure, I used to help fight off my dad on my mom as a child, but I was a young man now, full of untreated rage and in the vicinity of its root. I could not be there. I might have literally tried finally to kill him.

I stayed at Howard and took on more debt. It got better because I had come out, but a reality check of the consequences of my choices was looming. It took mere weeks after my college graduation to get it.

After I received my diploma, I immediately owed almost $800 a month in private loans, with twelve years to pay it off. That's not counting the few hundred dollars I still pay each month in federal loans. Fortunately, the government gave me more than twice the time to cough it up. Then again, they tack on a lot of interest, so fuck them, too.

Usually when someone attempts to discuss their student loan debt, their judgment is questioned.

How could I not have understood the financial commitment I was making? And if I'm so far in debt now, why am I writing this and not pursuing a more lucrative career as a doctor or lawyer—or, as one relative put it bluntly, "When are you going to work in a building?"

Know that if you are the type of person who asks these questions, I've got the gift of silence ready for you as soon as you send me an address.

I'm not dismissing my responsibility for this. But along with many other seventeen- and eighteen-year-olds, when I went to college I didn't know anything about student loans, interest rates, or rude private debt companies that hound the living hell out of you. All I knew was what I was told: College was *the* ticket to social mobility, and good students deserved to go to schools that matched their talent and ambition. Folks like me, who come from working-class backgrounds, were told to chase down a bachelor's degree by any means necessary. And then consider more. But no one mentioned just how expensive and soul-crushing the debt would be.

Still, I get it. I made the decision to take out loans. The voices in my head don't let me forget that. If they did, the people who call me in the wee hours on Sunday morning hoping to collect my outstanding balance in one lump sum will remind me, with great displeasure.

At my graduation, which took place on a beautiful day in May 2007, my commencement speaker and the best example of the intersection of auntie and deity to ever exist, Oprah Winfrey, spoke passionately on the toxicity of fear. "Don't be afraid," she told us. "All you have to know is who you are. Because there is no such thing as failure." I felt invigorated by her remarks when she delivered them. As I told everyone, while she delivered her remarks just being in Oprah's presence probably raised my credit score.

But once I got that congratulatory letter from Citibank, stating the terms of my debt and repayment, and understood it to be the financial equivalent of a backhanded compliment along with a dire warning not to play with them, panic took over. As the bank explained, my loan repayment plan only allowed two instances of six-month deferments. That was it. No more. In other words: I'd better run the bank its money *or else*.

I know it's blasphemous if not cosmically dangerous to ignore Oprah's wise words, but this was terrifying. I have lived in fear ever since. The greatest fear—the one that has controlled so many of my decisions—is that one day I may fall too far behind on payments, so much so that I will default on my loans, destroy my financial well-being, and take my mother down with me. That fear has given way to anxiety and depression—some periods more debilitating than others.

A couple years after that letter informed me of the grave mistake I had made—after I turned down an ideal first job for me because it wasn't going to allow me to live and pay my loans, after I moved back home and took whatever freelance jobs I could get to pay the bills and at least allow me to keep thinking everything I had done wasn't in vain, and after I moved to Los Angeles, where I once again had to turn down some opportunities in favor of the ones that allowed me to make as much money as possible to stay on top of those loans—I was driving around LA in a state of equal parts fury and despair. I called my cousin to tell her how sick of it all I was, that I was tired and couldn't take it anymore.

Then I turned off my phone. I needed silence. When I turned it on again a few hours later, I was greeted with frantic voicemail messages—back then, most people still checked those—including several from my mother. We had already had a difficult call the year prior, when I had that Hepatitis C scare that turned out to be a false alarm and a needless new example of how racism makes everything—including seeking competent medical attention—worse. Likely recalling the level of stress and angst in my voice at the time, though, she was terrified of what I might have done.

My brother also left a voicemail, trying to explain in his way why suicide was not the right option. He categorized suicide the way many do—as a cowardly act—and spoke exactly as a nigga from Houston would. I love him so much, but I didn't need to hear that shit. I called my mom back first, obviously.

"Ma'am, I had no intention of killing myself," I said. "I

would never do that to you, because you'd still be on the hook for these loans."

There's no relief for my wallet or my self-esteem. Every time I fork over another payment, I think about all of the other ways I could have financed my education. Why didn't I take more part-time jobs? I was in Washington—why didn't I try to date some closeted politician and be his well-compensated secret? Or spend more time at the campus gym and land a job stripping? I could have paid for classes in cash!

And for so long I took to heart the poisonous folklore about student-debt martyrs who selflessly scrape by to pay off their loans—those "I only ate Spam and paid off my $160,000 debt in ninety-six hours" stories. I blamed myself, thinking that if I had just worked harder and sacrificed more, I wouldn't be in this situation.

But the truth is, a lot of this was always out of my control. The student loan industry is a barely regulated, predatory system, and with Donald Trump in the White House and those equally useless people in Congress, oversight of the industry is becoming nonexistent.

I was trying to do the right thing for myself, and I believed that doing the right thing for myself would ultimately benefit my entire family. Despite the cost, going to the college I chose seemed like the best way to get to where I wanted to be. I understand now how naive I was; how uninformed I was; how my naiveté and my ignorance made me an easy mark for a predatory industry boosting a higher education system set up for us to fail.

I am a member of that class of college students that graduated into a financial crisis, not long after a 2005 bankruptcy bill was passed that made private student loans non-dischargeable unless borrowers could demonstrate that loan repayment put an "undue hardship" on their finances. Naturally, the undue-hardship exception has virtually never applied to anyone. It's so vague that it's virtually meaningless.

I think of that slippery little phrase every time I field a nasty phone call from my student loan oppressors. If only I were a corporation or a bank, privy to loopholes, tax havens, lenient bankruptcy provisions, and so many other measures that allowed it to be treated far more humanely than an actual human being. Like so many others, I'm muddling my way out of a trap. I try to accept that I'm simply doing the best that I can with the choices I made in earnest.

Whenever I think I am at that point when I have truly made peace with my choices, I am reminded again and again that I am not over the hump.

I got such a reminder in February 2018. It was months before the release of my first book, and I was doing everything in my power to get it as much attention as possible. Some of that included me writing an essay for the *New York Times* Sunday Review about my private loan debt woes. I ended it with what would prove itself to be a false sense of peace.

Recalling the more rude student loan payment callers, I boasted of a newfound ease with the struggle to continue making these sizable monthly payments, now well over a $1,000 a month in repayment bills: "the joy-inducing invention of that block button on the iPhone so that sometimes we can simply say, 'They'll get that money when I got it.'"

When I originally wrote these words, I really, really wanted to believe them. However, just two days before the essay went live, that peace I professed to have was hastily snatched away. I was told that unless I paid more than $800 before 8:00 mountain standard time the next day, I would default on my loans. For multiple reasons, I could no longer keep up with the payments and had fallen incredibly behind. Among them included having to do far less freelance work than I'm used to doing, in order to finish my book.

My first book was a lifelong dream, but it was a difficult journey in getting to that point. Part of what made it difficult was this belief that I was niche, and thus not deserving of what I felt was a fairer advance based on what I'd gleaned from colleagues. I am very much grateful for having a book deal with a major publisher, but I struggled so much through that. Still, I was hopeful. I convinced myself that this was just yet another sacrifice and that my better tomorrow was inching closer. I was determined to lean into the notion that life was about to become different for me. And that I'd earned that.

But when I made that payment and then learned the next morning that the customer service rep I had spoken with had taken out double the amount we agreed on, I was devastated. I was in the negative by several hundred dollars and with no income coming in soon enough to offset the error. Whenever you pay by phone with these people, they read aloud a verbal contract for every single amount you want to pay on a select loan (I had several, as they were divided largely by semester)—and then you say your full government name aloud. I am very familiar with this process. I did not pay online because I needed to pay specific amounts on individual loans in order to make sure none of them accidentally charged off ("charged off" means my loans defaulting, which for me would spell the end). I did exactly what I was supposed to, and someone else fucked up.

On the day I found out, I was making my first appearance on national television to talk about my book. The show was

The Opposition with Jordan Klepper. And yeah, that Sunday, this student loan essay was going to run in the Sunday Review of the *New York Times*. This was all a very big deal to some country boy from Houston who didn't know any damn body reading the *New York Times*, but loved the paper all the same because it often gave him a glimpse of what could be.

The day after that, I was due to appear in Philadelphia for my very first paid speaking gig. So much of work in media is doing free shit with the hope that one day you'll actually be compensated for your work. Most folks cannot afford this type of sacrifice, but we do what we have to do all the same.

In the invitation the World Affairs Council of Philadelphia, who hosted the event, extended to me, they noted that past guests included "almost every American President, Secretaries of State, Secretaries of Defense, and heads of state including Margaret Thatcher, Mikhail Gorbachev, Tony Blair, Sebastián Piñera, and Vicente Fox." And: "In the past two years alone, recent speakers have included Vice President Joe Biden, former General David Petraeus, Federal Reserve Board Chairwoman Janet Yellen, Supreme Court Justice Stephen Breyer, venture capitalist Daymond John, and author Tom Friedman."

And my Black ass. In this same fancy and formal letter, they cited my political articles with headlines such as "Someone Tell the Democrats to Stop Acting Like the Political Equivalent of Unseasoned Chicken." They knew what they were getting and they wanted me anyway. I was due to be in conversation with Andrew Sullivan about "tribalism." Any sensible soul would recommend air frying your tongue over speaking to Andrew Sullivan at length, but a check is a check.

I almost didn't get to earn the check from this gig, though, because I no longer had any money left and I needed money to get to Philadelphia. The organizers did not book my travel, but did say they would reimburse me. All I had was a little bit of credit on a card I had turned to for help while I tried to finish the book (further complicated by medical costs related to health issues spurred by stress—shocker). All of this was dawning on me as I was about to go on national television.

On the car ride down to the set, my hometown friend of more than twenty years, Jeanne, called me. Her teenage daughter was informing me that because I had a blue check by my name on Twitter, I was famous. That was comically false, but when she gushed about me and car service, I had to tell her to chill. I told her what was happening and how none of it mattered if I was struggling to eat.

She knew I was prideful. She knew how much I had already sacrificed. She could hear the pain in my voice. But she knew that I knew that I had to shake it off because I had to go be "on" because I had a book to shill for. You couldn't tell what was going on when you saw me on camera, but I immediately sank on the car ride back home.

That Sunday, I realized how incredibly difficult it was to find a physical copy of a newspaper—in Harlem, no less—and searched in vain to find a paper I actually couldn't afford to purchase because I needed to get through the feat of having food to eat in the next few days—so 'twas good that I couldn't find it and had to wait for my editor to mail me a copy. The next morning, I took a BoltBus to Philadelphia to debate identity politics with a condescending snob who deflected from every argument with hyperbole and theatrics. For example, did you know that Ta-Nehisi Coates and I are the "real racists"? Not sure if Coates had posted something that morning that drew Sullivan's ire, but FYI all the same. He went on to say that

I hated Catholics. Don't worry, he insulted the audience that included high school students, too. The night ended with him asking "Do you really think I haven't listened to a thing you said?" while going in for a hug before leaving the venue. I'd dismiss this as with all "white people," but there I go being the real racist again or something.

I think what mainly stuck with me in that moment was his insistence that most of the lingering barriers I spoke of were a figment of my imagination. Because he, who came from Britain, had managed to do all right for himself, it was some testament to his great American fable. It's adorable to believe we live in a meritocracy, but so much of certain types of success is dictated by everything else besides perceived special talents and abilities. It's about privilege, and how that privilege gives way to greater access and larger means than are offered those who lack it.

Those couple of days and the harder months that followed took such a toll on me. This was supposed to feel like the beginning of a triumphant transition. I was supposed to begin to feel the benefits of all those years of going without and struggling. Yet here I was doing some of the things I had long wanted to do and at the same time drowning in debt and so unstable that one mistake had made it extremely difficult for me to eat. How pitiful. How embarrassing.

Since finding out how much I would owe each month, there has not been a day in my life that I have not thought about my overwhelming debt. On many days, I decide to not let it dictate my day, that there's nothing I can do about it, so the best I can do is the best I can do. But then there are those darker moments when I think about how little control of my life I have allowed myself to have because of the choices I've made. And it's not about faulting or questioning anyone else. I'm glad Recruiter Bae instilled some optimism in me. It's a shame I have nowhere to send him a DM. I don't question my mom's choice to eventually give in to something she had said she wouldn't, but I have wondered if she regrets it.

She may no longer feel I'm a self-centered bastard for tagging this debt on both our backs. But I haven't always been so sure—and still wonder whether her words may continue to ring true.

FOR $1500 AN EPISODE

With the few friends to whom I mentioned the prospect, I always introduced it with the following caveat: "There is no fucking way that I am actually going to do this."

I just could not envision myself throwing house tequila and soda at some man I met through a casting director's imagination at some hookah spot in Harlem in the middle of the afternoon. Or crying inside of a church that looked as if it were roughly two more months of poor tithing away from turning into a chic fusion restaurant/lounge, one that only the new white neighbors and their Black friends who needed Black friends to tell them to fix their hair would frequent. My mama would never agree to appear on camera, so at least I wouldn't have to worry about the production capturing images of her swatting me with the New Testament as my dad poured more Paul Masson or Jack Daniel's into a water bottle. My hateful-ass friends would boo and hiss at such an assertion, but I'm kind of a classy-ass bitch now. Not a total class act (I used to love the 1992 movie entitled *Class Act* starring hip-hop duo Kid 'n Play), but someone that can sing Countess Luann de Lesseps's "Money Can't Buy You Class" and confidently bop to the line "elegance is learned, my friend."

A reality show would threaten that, among other things.

I love reality television as a viewer. And as a culture writer, I have written a lot about it. (Yeah, yeah, I'm fond of some of the "deeper" reality-centered pieces, but I'm proudest of my *Love & Hip Hop: Atlanta* recaps.) My appreciation for the genre notwithstanding, I knew there was a difference between being a proud consumer of the content and being an ideal candidate to help create it.

Yet here I was in a conference room for a meeting with a network, technically presenting myself as a cast member for a reality show. It had been a long year. The kind of year that makes you reevaluate your life and the choices you've been making. I may have kept consistently working as a freelance writer, but as many have come to learn or will learn in due time, one of the perils about the growing gig economy is that it can take you longer than it ever should for you to get paid for services rendered.

Years before *EBONY* magazine was sued by writers for unpaid work, I was stalking its accounts payable offices in Chicago. (I had warned some writers of the magazine's problems, but some choose to go where the work is even if there is a great risk attached—mainly because there is no work to be found elsewhere.) I was writing multiple times a week on the site, but not receiving regular checks. I had a pop culture and sex column in the magazine, too, but my check for that wasn't around either.

I wrote for other outlets, but sometimes they, too, had problems. Whereas some Black-owned publications struggled with capital, the white-owned outlets had been pumped with a lot of venture capitalist money that was often mismanaged—resulting in many a once highly trafficked outlet abruptly folding, and later being sold for far less than the overstated value it had coasted on. Already tired of not only this volume of work, but having to chase people for compensation, I was looking for something different. Something bigger, better, and less taxing. More than anything, something consistent.

Some opportunities were dangled in front of me, the sort that could help me ascend quickly, but none panned out fully, for various reasons—incompetence, gross mismanagement, small-mindedness, hater shit, what have you. Increasingly irritated, I was at the point where I asked myself whether or not it was time to sincerely consider taking an unexpected detour. Maybe it wouldn't take me exactly where I wanted to be, but if nothing else, perhaps it would take me out of this sad and sorry state that I felt stuck in.

I told myself from the very first conversation that I was just going to humor the process, maybe take notes for the future. That's not untrue, but it wasn't the curiosity alone that kept me around. It was also the rising fear that some of my goals might end up too far out of reach. *If I don't make any real headway soon.*

With my old dream of becoming Katie-Couric-with-a-dick long over, and my current setting of freelancer-who-wished-he-had-hoed-in-college-so-he-wouldn't-have-had-to-keep-taking-out-private-student-loans, I was now entertaining whether or not I ought to jump on the opportunity to become a more ambitious version of Shereé Whitfield.

Consider all of the athleisure clothes designed to wear at the club Shereé Whitfield could've moved on Instagram had she gotten She by Shereé off the ground while she still had a peach. If you are going to submit yourself to a medium that will lead to loss of anonymity (well, depending on the network, because some are more viewed than others) and likely doom you to encounter at least some nominal level of national embarrassment, you should do as much as possible to generate a profit from it with some business venture. If my storyline on *The Real Housewives of Atlanta* was centered on me becoming the Donatella Versace of Buckhead, as was the case for the self-described "Bone Collector," best believe my maxi dresses, tights, and denim designed for big asses (both natural and cosmetically enhanced to comedic levels of jiggle) would end up available for purchase. Not to take away from her accomplishments—getting Chateau Shereé up and running no matter whose name the utilities were in, Kenya Moore—but the time she had on the show could have been better spent hawking forever. In theory, I'd be in the confessionals sipping Casamigos with a metal straw (I'm so green), wearing a T-shirt with my book cover printed on it, commenting on a scene where I talked about designing organic thot briefs and notebooks bearing faux inspirational messages such as "My Heart Score > Credit Score."

If I did this, I would push harder than Shereé, which actually might make me more like Porsha Williams—but like if Porsha joined a good book club. I know that I'm not Nene Leakes because there is no way I could say "bridemaid" that many times on television without my tongue attempting to run away from home at least once. Regardless of which *Real Housewives* cast member was my true equivalent, the overall point is if you ever dare to do reality, you'd best have a plan on how to maximize the moment.

However, there were signs shouting "Run on, run on, Oprah" the entire time I kinda entertained this opportunity.

I found out about this through Dana, the boss of one of my editors at a site for which I used to write regularly. I was technically a freelancer, but the volume of daily work made it feel more like permalance. *Permalance* is a cute corporate term that loosely translates into "We are going to work you as if you were a full-timer, but we don't want to pay for your health insurance, so if you get sick, try some Robitussin or whatever it is you poor people use to treat yourselves because it's not on us."

When I met Dana, I immediately asked, "Gay men love you, don't they?" She wasn't a hag, just amazing. It was a compliment wrapped in a potential human resources violation.

Dana had an elevated taste level, as exhibited by the books, plays, films, and shows she mentioned. She was not someone I even assumed watched a lot of reality television, but she was also a realist: We both understood how you often have to meet people where they are—even more so when your plan is to take them from somewhere foreign to somewhere eventually satisfying.

When she first mentioned the show, she described it as an effort to show a group of gay Black men in the city not as we had been used to seeing them—i.e., as sidekicks and stereotypes alone. Yes, every producer talks like this, but I believed her intentions because I knew her and knew her vision came from a sincere place.

A lot of the jargon we hear from reality television's biggest personalities derives from the Black LGBTQ community. Many of us keep saying this with the hopes that at some point it will matter because it sucks to watch people bite and profit off it—especially when some of the very folks cashing in on our brilliance engage in casual homophobia with the best of them.

Dana wanted to put this group at the forefront, and while I had misgivings, I trusted her (and again, nothing else was happening, at least at the same pace). I never lost my trust in her, but it didn't take long to realize this was a collaborative effort in which not every collaborator shared a singular vision. When I went to a production office in order to shoot material for a reel, I noticed a whiteboard in front of me. It had the show name, a list of all the cast members, and some type of storyboard set for this scene they wanted to shoot for the pilot.

The scene in question curiously had my name in it, and below that was some note that referred to me having a disagreement with a person I had never met in my life. I know reality TV producers like to pit people against each other and stage settings to try and coerce real conflict out of people—so that folks like me will tweet about it—but damn. Could I meet somebody first before I was given too much alcohol to help me cuss them out better? Why was I already fighting people, anyway? Did I look angry? Was it the resting bitch face men—gay and progressive heterosexual alike—allegedly said I had?

Dana wasn't there when I saw this, so I never faulted her for it. Besides, I was familiar with the production company that was her partner. "Let Them Hoes Fight" isn't just an unreleased song with Trina and Lady Gaga, but a solid business model for that crew, so I figured this was their doing. Unsurprisingly, by the time I made it to their offices, most of the people originally attached to the project had fled.

I should have joined them, but I stuck around and ended up in that conference room for a meeting that felt like a Tyler Perry play got together with a hood lit novel written through a queer lens to troll me in front of white folks. It was such an interesting group of people assembled. I'm using *interesting* to be less of a bitch. That's actually why I invoked Shereé: Thanks to the gift that is self-awareness, I knew I wouldn't be a gossip like her, but I would more than offer an abundance of shade and free reads in my confessionals, with similar delivery.

I was certainly doing as much as I surveyed the conference room.

There was the stylist to stars I'd never heard of, practically tripping over himself to inform these television executives about the closeted married man whose dick he often sucked. He was definitely the kind of person who pulled out printed text messages at group gatherings.

There was the publicist to actual celebrities, a very nice man who appeared very much ready for his own moment. That was not a bad thing. I had seen him on television before.

There was the gay rapper who broke into a freestyle that had him sounding like vintage Lil' Kim, only if vintage Lil' Kim were simultaneously having an orgasm and a panic attack. I agreed with him that sodomy was totes lit, but if you're a rapper, you should at least try to make your musings on the subject rhyme. Then again, a lot of rappers born in the 1990s need Google Maps to direct them to the beat, so what do I know?

At the very end of the table was the handsome older man who had too great a résumé to even be in the room, which put him at odds with the rest of the cast. I think he filled the "daddy" role, and yes, I'm choking on my own vomit for writing that in a sentence.

Keeping with the theme of folks who didn't belong in this room, there was also me, sitting at the very end of the table, perplexed and vexed at what I was bearing witness to. I think my role on this would-be show was to be the "young" and "smart" one who had come to New York City to pursue his dreams of not dying a broke bitch in a fledgling industry with gross wage stagnation, wild uncertainty, and a bunch of people running what was left of it into the ground. I suppose I was Colored Carrie Bradshaw, post-recession.

The lead TV exec was a genial older white gay man who appeared to relish everything that was happening. Before we all did our introductions, he started with his. He shared that he was aiming to use this project as some kind of mission. As he explained to us, he hoped the show would cast light on the purported rampant homophobia in the Black community, as evidenced by the reactions his boyfriend's Jamaican family had had toward their lil' salt-n-pepa union.

No, you did not say that, white man.

When I did my introduction, I very southernly went, "My name is Michael Arceneaux, and respectfully, a lot of what I write about is against everything you just said about Black people." I was respectful in explaining why making Black folks the bogeymen of homophobia was inaccurate for a litany of reasons, backed up with readily available data. I later found out that this feedback was appreciated, but at the time, I couldn't wait to get out of that room. All of them surely noticed this.

I was never excited about doing a reality show, but like many people who are craving opportunities and have fears of dying in poverty, I considered the reality that there are only so many options for burgeoning gay Black male media personalities, so it behooved me to at least consider the "platform." But as much as I wanted an opportunity to be on camera, I wasn't thirsty for just any opportunity. Certainly not one that appeared likelier to result in me turning into an example of one of the very essay topics I routinely covered—tropes about gay Black men.

With that lingering uneasiness now for sure not going away,

I turned for guidance to someone who knew a thing or two about big career transitions. Or someone I figured, better yet, would confirm my suspicions and lovingly guide me back to my original path. She was someone who had left her corporate career behind and gradually become the television personality she aimed to be. But she had specifically not turned to reality television in order to do so, and she did not mince words about finding it to be a foolish path for me to follow.

She was as always, fun, but when it came to broaching this subject, curt out of concern.

Name someone from reality television who successfully transitioned out of reality television into some of the more serious interests you've previously told me about.

Actually, just name someone out of the world of reality TV period that managed to transition out.

Bethenny Frankel.

Bethenny Frankel. You niggas always say Bethenny Frankel. You are not no fucking Bethenny Frankel.

Mind you, this was before Bethenny Frankel's talk show was canceled and she took her Skinny Girl Margarita–slinging ass back to *The Real Housewives of New York* (thank you, Bethenny). Either way, no, I was not no fucking Bethenny Frankel.

What are you going to do? Talk about how you were afraid to have sex because you didn't want to die of AIDS for $1500 an episode? That's what you think is going to make your career?

Sometimes love comes from a dragging. I was being lovingly scolded and I appreciated every second of it. It was like the angel on one side of my body flying over to stab the demonic thing on the other side.

As much as I'd like to say it was her compliments about my

intelligence, talent, and potential that finally steered me away from charting a new path as Shereé-Whitfield-if-she-tried-harder, I was mostly stuck on the fact that she was right about me potentially showing my whole ass for pennies on the dollar. If I was going to allow a production crew the right to chop and screw my image into one of their making, I should definitely be making Equinox money. Fifteen hundred dollars an episode didn't feel like that when you factored in New York, everything else, plus my student loans. (And I wasn't sure that if this shit really happened I'd even be earning that much.) This network was cute, but like Burlington Coat Factory in a white neighborhood, it might have yielded a few cute items, but it was still all discounted and slightly irregular, beloved. Publishing money ranged as low as sneaking into Planet Fitness because you wanted some of that free pizza that's been sitting out there the whole damn day.

I later found out that following the meeting, the network folks said they liked my personality but wanted to know more of my "story." That just meant I hadn't told them enough mess to exploit. Forgive me for not having grabbed fidelity by the dick and sucked it, even though I knew it was married, because I hoped to one day rap about it in front of a white liberal. Clearly, I didn't feel like channeling my inner E. Lynn Harris novel, so I left it alone.

Some time after that, I was told that the direction of the show was changing.

Instead of being focused on the lives and careers of gay Black men, it would be about gay men and their besties. Even better, the besties were actually now the focus of the series; the gay friends were relegated back to sidekick status. The whole point of the show had been to do something atypical for television, so of course television executives rushed to stop that from happening. It never made it to air. And that was just as well because I had already run free from it.

In the end, I'm glad that didn't work out. I got approached for another reality project a little over a year later. I can't recall their official log line, but I got *The Real Homosexuals of Cardi B's Internet* teases. No thank you.

My attitude about gay Black men's participation in the genre—how it should look, how it should not look—has changed since that ordeal. While I want to help diversify the images of queer Black men in mass media, much like the images of Black people more broadly, it's important that we see variety— because we *are* varied people. Entertainment does not necessarily have to enlighten. In other words, I need to be mindful of what is presented before me and challenge gross distortions when necessary, but you know, watching a bunch of gay Black folks acting a fool on a reality show is fine.

In the same way I realize pristine images of Black people will not automatically make the ignorant less intolerant, I know that the same can be said of queer Black folks. I don't want the support of those who generalize.

Also, *Moonlight* happened, and a few months after it won Best Picture at the 89th Academy Awards, a digital series about a group of Black LGBTQ folk living in Atlanta premiered on YouTube.

Chasing Atlanta is a show following a gaggle of gay Black men pursuing their dreams in the big city. Most of the men who make up the original cast are out of their damn minds. I have never met someone who purposely introduced themselves as a "socialite" without being sarcastic, but thanks to this show, I am reminded that the folks on Instagram who list themselves as "socialites" in their bios truly mean that shit. It's so embarrassing but, with a camera crew, enticing.

By natural order, the other jobs listed (both real and imagined) included the usual suspects who wanted nothing more than to be famous. A chef. A model. An actor. A designer. A choreographer. An artist. I'm surprised there wasn't an artist who used to model but planned to perform for a while before taking on acting full-time, then retiring and releasing a cookbook.

Having said that, I am a gay dude that writes for a living, so who am I to judge anyone else for being a cliché?

But even as it sounds like I'm reading them—okay, I kind of am, but hear me out—I am also exalting them because they give me jubilee. They act just like every other batshit crazy person I enjoy on reality television—but they happen to be men whom I might spot in an Atlanta club on a Saturday night after I was given an edible and promised that I could pregame at Pappadeaux. That makes it special.

Chasing Atlanta is a Bravo show with a public access budget. Does that make it WeTV? Please advise.

When I say smaller budget, I mean on its series premiere, the cast meets up in a hotel room that viewers strongly believe is at an area Howard Johnson. There is nothing wrong with booking a room at a Howard Johnson, but Bravo should be able to do better. The same with the cast going on a camping trip at what kind of looks like a rest stop along the interstate. When they are making s'mores, it looks like it was filmed with an iPhone 7.

All of this is what makes the show all the more impressive to me. Yes, the show isn't working with a big budget, but the production on it deserves kudos all the same. Their music supervisor is on point. As is the graphics person. Round of applause to their MacBooks for doing the most with what they were given.

The biggest applause, though, goes to the cast for being so entertaining. They all remind me of gay Black men I have seen across the South. They even argue about the same kind of dumb shit, too.

On season one of the show, Jaylon is beefing with Devon over the fact that Jaylon feels Devon doesn't look like his picture on one of the apps. Seriously, that is their beef for the entire season. Petty as it sounds, people do drag those who look like their face was run through seven and a half filters and a gas station car wash.

Jaylon is in a deep committed relationship with the word "boss." I have never heard someone say "boss" so many times in my life as I have by this person on this show. As noted, I'm Black, so that means something. The rest of them will tell you that they are all bosses, too. Not as much as Jaylon, but still. If you told them that they couldn't say "boss" for a month, the show would be a silent film. In future seasons, the cast diversifies to include trans women, and the arguments become more inclusive as well—introducing new participants like stun guns. I do not endorse violence, but I can appreciate an emphasis on realism.

There is now a spinoff, *Chasing Dallas*. As a native Houstonian, I have an inherent anti-Dallas bias, but with age comes grace, so please let the record show that I think it's cute for something that takes place . . . in Dallas.

Someone on the show introduces himself as "a socialite, fashionista, and everybody knows my name." I don't know him. One guy is a "stylist to the elite." Heard it all before, Little Miss

Sunshine Anderson. Another guy is a makeup artist, or as he puts it, "the RuPaul of faces." I'll never know what that means, but if nothing else, it got me to pause and think about it for a few seconds.

Another guy is a trainer who specifically gets folks to have small waists and fat asses. As legend has it, his man told him he got too big, so he got IG fine. That man is apparently now gone. Men ain't shit, but his ass is quite nice. Salute to the cheeks shaped by shame but now sitting high in self-confidence.

Another cast member is married but doesn't want that to stop anyone from sliding into his DMs. It's fascinating to know of a young Black gay married couple (although the husband does not appear), but what is most intriguing is the manner in which this cast member confidently explains their lifestyle and how it works for them.

The following are some notable quotables from *Chasing Dallas*:

"Since he don't have any furniture in his apartment."

"Where is your platform?"

"Do I give fish?"

"I was giving Beychella realness."

"We apologize for the audio in this scene."

They don't say "boss" as much as in their inaugural season. They are more "secure the bag" homos. On one episode, in noting the apparent rift between the gay and straight communities, a cast member hosts a "unifying event" featuring Hennessy and fried chicken. I might have gone if invited. *Chasing Dallas* does offer a scant amount of seriousness—specifically one cast member revealing that he is dealing with a meth addiction before leaving the show to deal with it.

Altogether, the show has generated hundreds of thousands

of views, which should be applauded but begs the question: Why aren't these folks and all their ridiculousness on my TV yet? Why are they still only on the internet and YouTube?

If I can hear straight cisgender white men use "shade" on morning news stations and, well, Black women unleash a flurry of our jargon on numerous reality shows, why can't I see the people who reflect the community that created it all cashing in, too? I should be able to see this chicken fried steak with steak sauce soap opera starring Black queer fame chasers.

The rebooted *Queer Eye* is genuinely lovely and I appreciate how it makes viewers—notably those who don't interact with my kind—feel, but that's not enough for those who don't necessarily need to be enlightened while being entertained. I don't want to see just fairy god queers who can extend to Trump supporters the humanity their votes deprive the most vulnerable of. I want to see mess, too.

Did I want to be on a show like this a few years back? No. Would I do it now? Fuck no. But would I host their reunions? Absolutely.

I'm sorry for my previous insult, WeTV. Can you put them on?

Yes, I can see it on YouTube every week, but they deserve more. I doubt they even get $1500 an episode for sharing so much of themselves. They probably get club bookings to compensate, the way other reality stars do, but that, too, feels imbalanced because queer clubs aren't working with the same level of capital. How could they? Most of us are not getting paid the kind of compensation that reflects our work.

I've learned this lesson over and over again throughout my life, but the reminder I got navigating this experience will forever be hard to top. My brief flirtation with reality television was borne out of frustration, and in hindsight, mild desperation, but it didn't take long for me to recognize this wasn't the best move for me to make. I strongly believe that if I'm going to throw a plate of fried crab dumplings at a coworker, and maybe right after the table it was placed on, and embarrass myself, it should come with a nice check. I can enjoy other people making a mess of themselves, though, and if you're out there leasing your likeness to television producers for your come up and your entertainment value to us, thank you for your services.

And I hope you are being properly compensated.

QUIT PLAYING ON MY PHONE

The calls typically come as early as 7 a.m. EST and as late as 9 p.m. EST. Occasionally, though, they may give me a ring a little later than that—or too damn early. I will never forget being in Houston for the holidays and my phone going off a little after 6 a.m. I remember this so well because it took place on Christmas Eve, a day people of more elevated sensibilities would conclude is better served leaving people be. Even if the person calling doesn't go up for Jesus's b-day, and capitalism's wildest orgy, 'tis the season to chill out on matters such as these. Or so I would like to think.

She sounded so cheery on the phone. Who calls someone to harass them about late student loan payments with such a disposition that early in the day on the cusp of the biggest holiday of the year? We're about to celebrate the birthday of Jesus! You don't remind people of their debts until at least the third day of Kwanzaa. She must have been a sociopath on her third cup of coffee.

I should not have picked up, but I didn't want to be bothered throughout the day with her calling me again. So we talked. Well, I purposely dominated the conversation in an effort to say my piece and hoped she'd land on the position that now wasn't the time to keep badgering me.

Yes, this is Michael.

Yes, I understand why you are calling, but as I explained to one of your colleagues a few days ago, I don't know when I will be able to make another payment.

However, I did make sure to make a payment last week to avoid charge off.

She granted me mercy by informing me that she would make sure the calls would cease for a few days. They were back on December 26. I should have known better—I was told during last week's call, too, that I would get a reprieve. Here we were, all the same.

I guess thirty-six hours of space is better than none.

The first time I got one of these calls, I was mortified. Me? Behind on a payment? No, no, no. I was not going to be one *of those*. That is not a diss to people who fall behind on payments—millions upon millions of people living in America (and counting). Life happens; that I get. But I didn't want it to become a regular thing for me. It would mean that I was losing my fight to stay afloat of this debt. That would then mean that it was having an impact on my credit. And if it was having an impact on my credit, it would hurt me if I wanted to get a car, a house, one of those credit cards that can lead to racking up points so that I could take a damn vacation somewhere nice without having to come out of pocket as much. Beyond all of this, not being hounded by creditors was just its own peace of mind. I was determined not to lose mine.

Whatever needed to be done, whatever needed to be

sacrificed, to make sure those payments were made on time was done. I operated this strictly for a significantly long time. As I said, I was determined.

Then things became harder than they needed to be. One company owed me so much money during the summer of 2014—well over $5,000—and that spilled into the fall. Whatever else I brought in had to go to necessities. I was living check to check and constantly trying to collect as many of them as possible. And when your financial state is stuck in quicksand, it's easy to slip and bust your ass on the ground. So here I was.

It got a little better, but it was so easy to fall back behind. The system was designed this way. I hated to feel like a statistic, some sob story. But life became more about mere survival than appeasing the people making my life a never-ending financial nightmare. Or, when I miraculously had the chance, helping other people through their own financial distress. My loans may have been devastating to me, but I had grown up seeing far worse devastation. So I helped when I could. It has become easier to ignore my student loan oppressors over time because there are only so few people I ever actually speak to on the phone. That, and the robocalls are endless; I let the *ignore* and *silent* options on my iPhone serve their purpose. I assume no one means to call me unless the conversation has been previously scheduled or a blood relative over the age of forty needs to voice their distress. But eventually—unfortunately—I do have to make contact. So when I am good and ready, as my pops would say, albeit in a more financially solvent context, I dial that number. By *good and ready*, I mean when I am either prepared to make good on how much I owe in back payments, or if too many media entities owe me paychecks at once, I want to find out the bare minimum I need to pay to avoid defaulting on any of my loans. It's not that big of a choice for me in the end: *Settle up or snuggle up with your nightmare scenario.*

They call my mother, too. She did cosign these loans—against her better judgment. In fact, they call her as much they call me. She's become immune to this; she's learned to ignore them. I hate that I have put her in the position to be harassed in that way. Every so often she will send me a text saying she picked up the phone and gave them some amount of money. She says not to worry about it. I tell her thank you, but that I wish she hadn't given them anything. After all, she brought me up in Catholicism, so she should know that I can't shake off guilt easily.

Yes, we could change our numbers, but that really doesn't solve the underlying problem, now does it, beloveds? The debt is still the debt. Besides, to completely ignore a major financial institution to which you owe a large debt would be inciting the wrath of a major financial institution. I'd rather not.

Once I engage any of these people on the other end of the line, I get right to it. I give them my name and my Social Security number. They ask me to wait a moment for their computers to update. Then they ask would I like to pay the total outstanding balance?

I try not to laugh. *Do you think I called to give you that much? If I did, I would have paid online, fool. No, this call is to perform damage control with what I have to offer. But cute of you to be that optimistic given your line of work.*

I give just enough to avoid default. Just enough means, at minimum, $800 or so. But there are the times when the loan companies hear me say the word "no," and their voices shift to a disappointed tone. If they are genuinely nice people or new to their jobs, they will ask if I would like to explore the options available to me during times of financial hardship. I assume when my name appears on their computer screen, there is some indication that no such options exist. Something along the lines of "this bitch is hopeless, but he better pay us." But apparently not, because I have to inform them that no such options exist. Sometimes, they'll offer to check just in case. They then return and confirm what I already knew to be true.

Then I get asked why I have fallen behind on payments. The question enrages me every single time, but I have to maintain my composure. On second thought, no, I often do not, but I try not to be rude to people who haven't been rude to me. It's not because I fear they will hear the Lawry's seasoning in my voice and fall into stereotypes about Black people. I couldn't give any less of a fuck about that. If they want to believe the worst, white people will think whatever they want about Black people no matter the setting, income, credit score, or debt ratio. So it's not that at all. I just try not to be rude. It's the southerner in me. My problems are not the fault of any of them—something I tend to say when trying to answer their frustrating line of questioning in an effort to get to the point and go on about my day.

Freelance writing and my various other hustles, which all fall under the scope of contract work, don't make my life easier, but at the same time, I've come to realize that even if I was a W-2 bitch (a term of endearment, I assure you, W-2 bitches) earning an obscene amount of money, life wouldn't necessarily be any better for me. It is a pain to be paid late and to have to essentially threaten to run up (legally or physically), but with experience, you learn to better bob and weave with those companies that take longer than they should.

The underlying issue is that I am required to pay an enormous sum of money per month by most American workers' standards—all while simultaneously trying to eat regularly and not be homeless.

So, that's why I'm late, motherfuckers, and while I understand that none of the people who answer the phone are in control of their employers' policies, they should all acknowledge that by not offering to negotiate repayment terms under any circumstances, the whole system makes the situation all the more difficult. For them and for me.

I did try to refinance once. Very early on, actually. What ended this was noticing that, at the time, most of those companies offering refinancing were trying to fuck me over even worse. One company in particular made an offer to somehow expand my debt from a twelve-year repayment structure to a thirty-year one without decreasing the monthly payments by any significant figure. I stuck with the devil I had come to know.

What kills me about each and every one of the customer service reps from Citibank Student Loans and eventually Discover Student Loans (the former sold my debt to the latter) is that they are keenly aware of how screwed I am in the situation. You want me to pay $800 a month on a twelve-year plan with only two deferments? This sum on top of other bills—including some other student loans that covered expenses these other loans did not? In the United States of America? And not as a millionaire?

That's what makes their repeated inquiries so frustrating.

But their questions end up asked and answered.

Once I wrap my remarks, the people on the phone proceed to stop pretending they can be helpful and accept my payment.

They *know* that there is no additional deferment available unless there is a natural disaster that significantly affects where you live. Likewise, they are fully aware that their employer, my lender and oppressor, will not lower my payments in favor of an extended repayment period.

I hate cyclical conversations generally, but I loathe none more than these.

Annoying as they are, I can at least deal with the well-meaning folks. A few of them even reference their own student loan woes. And again, they didn't do this to me. Their employer did—and only has the ability to do so because I gave them consent once I took their money. My not totally understanding what I was getting myself into is now not a productive thing to fixate on. You can't go back. As much as I strive not to care about what others think of me, the less-than-nice bill collectors do get to me.

All that said, even if I understand people have a job to do, and even if I have no intention of being rude to people over my struggles with my student loan debt, that doesn't mean I want to talk to any of these people. Who cares if they're cordial in conversation when they're still calling me early in the morning and late into the night? Or when I'm heading to a funeral or when I'm in the middle of tears about a loved one suddenly passing? Or when I'm at the movies? Or at a restaurant? Or when it interrupts my Friday night and I have to excuse myself to go into a room and give up literally the last of what I have in order to avoid defaulting? These callers may not be fully aware of what a Draconian process this all is and how they play a role in it, but does that make it any less of a nightmare for me? No, so all the more reason to especially hate the callers who go out of their way to be disrespectful.

It has been my experience that no matter who they are with regards to their gender or race and ethnicity, if they are the type of person who thinks they are above someone struggling to make their payments, they will make that evident to you.

Many of them seem to derive joy from kicking another person when they're down. What a peculiar kind of twitch. I assume that it makes them feel better about their own short-comings. Or they're just assholes that arguably should have been swallowed. I can't call it, I just catch it the second I get a whiff of it. It's not like they make it hard to. They want me to know they think less of me.

Sometimes I give it back to them. To make clear that my struggles with this one facet of my life do not mean I am what-ever caricature of a broke person they have conjured in their minds (as they sit in a cubicle, more than likely making a lot less than I do). In a few instances, my words to them involve lots and lots of profanity. It doesn't make me feel any better, and I'm sure it doesn't help their day. Oh, well. They should learn to live by the proverb *Don't start no shit, won't be no shit*— and making people suffer through student loan repayment is the *most flagrant* example of starting shit.

They remind me of the most terrible sect of TSA employ-ees. The ones who take even the slightest bit of newfound power and start behaving like mini-tyrants since it's as close proximity to that level of control as they'll ever get. The power trippers who smugly speak down to people going through security, the ones that you want to chop in the throat but can-not, because the last thing you want is to get tackled at the se-curity checkpoint and taken into federal custody. Or any club bouncer. Why do so many of them act like assholes? It's not our fault they didn't make the cut for the NFL, the WWE, or UFC. Anyone who exists within this subgenre of humanity ranks high among the most contemptible. The bill collectors for the student loan oppressor are the Kevin and Joe to their Nick.

Whenever I get caught up on my payments, I feel such a great sense of relief, though it lasts for only a short while. It doesn't take long for me to worry all over again. About what happens if I fall behind once more. When I get the sneaking suspicion that I might, my anxiety levels start to rise. The breaths become louder and sharper as my mind wrongly convinces itself that the air will soon escape me altogether.

Part of that is knowing that no matter how long I go with consistent payments—ranging from a few months to several months to well over a year—the calls will sound the same no matter what.

It is technically better to speak to a sympathetic ear than an unsympathetic one, but I wish I didn't have to talk to these people at all. These calls have taken a mental toll on me over time. I am uneasy with that admission—yes, it's pride—but it is one reached for reasons that feel reasonable.

For more than a decade now, whenever I have fallen behind on student loan payments that rival mortgage payments across various parts of the South and Midwest, I know that I will be inundated with calls hour after hour every single day of the week (yes, sometimes on Sunday morning, too) badgering me about the impossible situation I have to live with. Yeah, some of them will behave decently; offer condolences for my situation and wish me luck. And yeah, some of them will put me down; go out of their way to make me feel worse than I already do. They're all villains to me, no matter their tone.

They're all reminding me of my failures and my hardships and how both are rooted in a mistake I made in 2002 when I sought the assistance of a bank to fund my college tuition. I did not know I basically was sacrificing myself to a poorly regulated system designed to help major corporations fuck suckers over. It's a mistake I can't take back.

The feeling won't go away until they go away. They will not go away until I pay them off. I used to say that on the day I make my last payment to my student loan oppressors, I would hand deliver the check and proceed to piss on the grass outside of the building if not the building itself. I wanted to hold a press conference, too. I imagine this would have ended up in my being asked to leave private property by a member of law enforcement who may or may not have shot me in the face for no other reason than it being a Black one, but the goal was to troll them as hard as they have trolled me if only for mere moments. I have hated these people for so long. For very good reason.

Now that I'm getting older, I'm not angling to tempt fate in that way. I won't show up at the corporate headquarters, knucking and bucking and ready to fight. I won't channel my inner Al Sharpton and pop my collar at the podium in the pursuit of some justice. All I want is peace. I cannot wait to take comfort in knowing that those people can never call me again. That I won't have to deal with any of those nosy people thinking they are Suze Orman or some shit. Or the people who act like they are some oligarch calling me from their lofty apartment in a Trump Tower they may or may not be using to launder money, allegedly.

I cannot wait to have the peace that comes from knowing they can never call me again. I am almost there. I won't think

I'm better than anyone for it, either. I only hope they never have to experience that burden, and if they do, that they are freed from it, too. But if they call you at the crack of dawn on Christmas Eve or on the weekend, I'll always defend your right to cuss them smooth out.

K STREET THOT
(AND OTHER CAREERS CONSIDERED)

I always forget LinkedIn exists until someone I met once seven years ago sends me a request to "connect." For what purpose? I heard from straight people that the business-casual hussies (this is a gender-neutral term round this way) use LinkedIn not to network but to hook up. Hard pass (double meaning intended). I prefer for any consensual sexual trysts that begin in a DM to be initiated on a platform that is not permanently set to business casual. And I write for a living. If you need to connect with me for work, scour my Twitter timeline mid-rant and send an email asking if I want to write eight hundred words for middling-to-good money (depending on the outlet), like any other editor in this climate.

But then I have to remember that there are much better adults than I am out in the world who use LinkedIn to network and/or nut. And they want their connection. Like, they really, really want that connection. So whenever I decide to finally respond to the seventy-second email reminding me that a person from wherever I met them wants to connect and then never speak to me again, I am on the site, and soon thereafter, reminded of what could have been.

Instead of listing "writer," which continues to be not a real job to sizable portions of the population for reasons both valid and totes unfair, my job title should perhaps be "senior medical analyst." Or "pharmacist." Or "investment banker." Or whatever screams *responsible, stable adult with ample amounts of disposable income that no private student loan could conquer.*

Believe me, I am fully aware of the fun fact that choosing a career in media was not the wisest option for someone interested in not feeling swallowed whole by their sizable debt. I did not go in with blinders. I understood that I would be required to perform a lot of indentured servitude guised as an internship before even being considered to get hired for my first low-paying entry level position. I also knew that it would take time to overcome the seemingly endless sacrifices made in order to eventually get over that hump. These positions are primed for people with means. People who can actually afford the sacrifice. It's cute when folks who *are* of means like to go on and on about how hard they work, but while no one can take away whatever strong work ethic they claim to have, they still have a leg up.

My mom's nursing career saw her begin as an LVN rather than the higher-earning RN she wanted to be before entering nursing school. Determined, well over a decade later, she made the choice to go back to school while raising kids to get her RN and make more for her family. In both of my parents, I saw people with multiple hustles doing whatever was required to get by and work for a better way for their children. I had reason to think I could do the same for my own dream.

What I did not count on was graduating during the worst economic conditions since the Great Depression and an entire industry blindsided by a swift and ultimately fatal shift from print to digital at the advent of faster internet. When I graduated, I was willing to take whatever role was close enough in proximity to get the start I needed. It took some time, but I did get one offer to be the assistant to the editor in chief of a publication I grew up obsessing over. I initially took it, only to turn it down because I didn't think it was enough to cover my student loan payments, which were already set at about $800 a month. I have mentioned that tidbit previously, but what I leave out is that I really, really wish I hadn't listened to the advice of the person who told me to *turn it down, stay home.*

I blame no one but myself for whatever choices I make, but what I would say in hindsight is that the best counsel comes from people who understand not only the way you think, but the way a given world is. I can't listen to folks who don't know the world I'm trying to enter as I learn it on the fly. People may have your absolute best intentions at heart, but dreams often die at the encouragement of those who have long since let theirs die.

Pragmatism has immense value, but in this case it came from the place of basically saying, *Well, you went to college for X, Y happened instead, so I C your Black ass better figure some other shit out fast 'cause ain't nobody rich round this way.* The argument had merits, but it felt unfair to portray my yearning for a life I had always pictured for myself in spite of setbacks and reality checks as a selfish act. It wasn't selfish; it was keeping me alive.

Now, for inquisitive minds near and dear, of course I have considered other careers outside of writing. Before it was Trump's America, it was Barack Obama's America, and before that, George W. Bush's America, and before that, Bill Clinton's America, and before that, George H. W. Bush's America, and before that, Ronald Reagan's America, the one I was born in. The pain ratio varies by the plutocrat and neoliberal, but the constant with each era is that if you are a Black person living in America, unless you come from a sweet, sweet cushion—the rarest of scenarios for the demo—you have to be prepared for the worst because you are typically dealt the harshest circumstances.

I may not have the best schooling, but a bitch is only slightly blind, not dumb, and while I'm not deaf, I really need to turn down the volume on my headphones at the gym.

The following are several other career options outside of media and entertainment that I have contemplated or been encouraged to pursue over time. Some are signs of desperation; others suggest I need to switch strains. Some are opportunities that have come to me directly and randomly; others are suggestions used in language that loosely translates into "stop being a masochist."

Most are no longer in consideration, but you never know. Again, I'm a Black. I live in the United States of Wage Stagnation and Economic Inequality.

CAPITALIST

My mother and I have an undeclared ritual with respect to my airport travel. It goes as follows: she always picks me up from the airport and she always takes me back to the airport.

It matters not what happens in between each visit so long as how I arrive and how I depart remain the same. It's the way it is, and no, I'm not thinking of Keyshia Cole after reading that; your hood, R&B-loving ass is! It has been this way since I was eighteen years old and left for my matriculation at Howard University, tacking on a debilitating degree of debt that would go on to have an impact on every facet of my life the very second my second deferment ended.

There was only one time she did not pick me up: when I went to Houston for a book event. Given the sensitivity toward me writing about being a practicing homosexual and telling the masses my business (one of the gravest of sins to a southern Black woman who grew up with the Bible era and not the blogging era), I broke tradition that time and rented a car at the airport to spare us both a disaster.

It bothered me for a lot of reasons, but mostly because what I love most about those to and from rides to the airport is that it is *our time*. I use a lot of that time to ask how she is doing with work (or I used to, before she retired). Then I get updates on the extended family members I love and cherish—and also the ones I haven't seen since 2Pac died or Rick Ross dropped "Tupac Back"—and likely won't bother seeing again unless 'Pac's ghost visits me in a dream demanding as much on a day when I'm feeling generous.

For my mom, this is her chance to *be* a mom, which for many, many, many, many moms is a chance to tell their special little miracle how they can salvage their mess of a life. My mom, longtime lover of the Lord, of course brings up why I ought to return to the church. She's never been like "GO BACK TO CHURCH NOW, MY SODOMITE SON!" but that's only because southern women know how to wield their might in a way as soft as their biscuits. Of course, she inevitably brings up Jesus and church in our car rides, but her delivery has gotten softer.

She's long given up making pointless references to a wife and kids, because neither of us is getting any younger, so why waste any second that could go elsewhere?

We both talk about my career, or better yet, I try to explain why I am not a failure—though she doesn't necessarily believe me to be a failure, but rather someone who needs to make a lot more money and probably could if they found another way to make it other than writing. One time, after we made our first and second post-airport stops—Shipley's, for the best donuts and kolaches ever, and Whataburger, for all the fixings I've been missing while up yonder in New York—we were riding down South Post Oak and there were only a few minutes left before our ride time was set to end. As I ate my jalapeño sausage and cheese kolache in the passenger side of my mama's ride, my mom said something about maybe me working in finance. Or something about business. An MBA? Whatever sounds like *The Wolf of Wall Street* without the prison time. (I have never seen *The Wolf of Wall Street*, but assume this is one of the few times a white man will go to jail for a financial-related crime, because clearly it's a much harder feat to net in real life.)

This wasn't the first time she'd mentioned me doing some kind of job that centered on the mo-mo-money, the yen and the pesos. While I was in college, probably about midway and not too late to save myself from a communications degree in this economy, my mom threw out a few suggestions on how the rest of this journey should go: something about my pledging a fraternity and me working in finance or law since I'm so obsessed with the words and things. I can't recall a direct mention of a vagina and vaginal sex, but I'm sure it was intimated at the time. Ever the good son in my head, I briefly considered each thing. Finance is probably the thing I'd be the worst at, but would benefit most from.

I've seen footage of Ebenezer Scrooge, the early years. I watched *DuckTales* religiously and saw Scrooge McDuck swim through that gigantic vault full of gold in the opening theme. I recall that before he became president, Donald Trump was paraded around as Richie Rich after his balls dropped and got stuck halfway. Believe me, I understood the perks of being a rich business type early in life.

Unfortunately, only Beyoncé can get away with not knowing much about algebra. Like, I am a failure of the Houston Independent School District. Creatives aren't often known for being math whizzes, but couple that with a few fun facts about my educational background: When I started ninth grade, our algebra teacher, Mr. Whomever, apparently died right before the school year started. In his place was an uncertified fill-in who was pregnant and looked two finished pickles away from her water breaking. She ended up lasting a bit longer than expected, but do you know what I remember most from that class? This one dude who played football having the nicest ass and a classmate I had known since elementary school teaching some other girl how to hide a razor under her tongue. The next year was somewhat better, but the inconsistency in quality of teaching left me with, uh, quite a wake-up call once I got to college.

I managed to get my degree, but yeah, my math abilities are nonexistent, so if I could go back in time, I would fix my mathematics journey by way of actual learning and retaining of what I had been instructed. And maybe I would at least give vaginal sex a real try for my mom's sake. Just kidding, I would have run track and kept the track body as much as possible until I found a sponsor—preferably a successful financial analyst, venture capitalist, or any other job title Bernie Sanders would rightly assert is ruining the fabric of society or whatever.

I would have been far more philanthropic than them, though.

K STREET THOT

Some of the gays like to put down sex work, but from a viewer's perspective, the escorts who sell ass successfully usually seem happier than those judgmental sissies (I can say it), so with respect to shame, the label feels misplaced. Regardless, I have wondered whether or not my time at Howard could have been better spent on Capitol Hill or K Street, where power really likes to party (no capitalized T 'cause meth ain't it). Not only could I have gotten my tuition paid, I could have gotten the loans I took out my freshman year paid for. And maybe an off-campus apartment. While we're at it, a car, too, 'cause everybody knows the Metro is some bullshit.

Now, I'm not saying I would have been slobbing lobbyist and/or congressional knob, Alhamdulallah. Again, most dicks are ugly, and I'm selective, which is a classier way of saying selfish and suspicious. My earning potential would have been higher, but there are only so few attractive people in politics, and these types are the ones who pay them, not the other way around. Life can be cruel, etc.

So I would have elected to be something of a boy toy. It would have required me to presumably only eat kale, açaí, and bun-deprived turkey burgers, but no debt? To quote the late

Macho Man Randy Savage, "Ooh yeah, dig it!" Same goes for working out to an obnoxious level that resulted in one of the tricks paying for my trainer. That also would have been fine because it sounds very *Real Housewives*—only in secrecy because most of these types are married to a woman.

I would have accompanied the men—varying from dirty old man to sad older gay man who's actually not that bad but is painfully socially awkward—to social events most people of any age would find boring but I would relish because I am basically an endless stream of political commentary. The attendees, white . . . duh . . . would have been pleasantly surprised by my political awareness because the least is expected of the young and Black in these circles. They would have been intrigued by my hair because unlike a lot of the Black men in the world of politics as active players or storytellers, my line-up actually exists.

This would have lasted until graduation and ended with one of those folks blessed to have enjoyed my company (albeit with invoicing attached) hooking me up with a great entry-level pushing.

This would have been a great scam, only it never came to pass because I grew up deathly afraid of dying of AIDS and programmed to think homosexuality was an abomination. Actually, whatever to that because plenty of people have that problem. My issue is it took me too damn long to get over the shit. Had I known by at least twenty that Jesus Christ truly doesn't give a damn where I stick it, I could have made this plan work—especially after someone sent me a clue about my lender's repayment plan. I know this because later in life I met someone who effectively served as an intermediary between college boys and men who pay for their company.

I could have been a Sugar Baby!

. . . or not.

I'm far too self-aware, so as much as it sucks to admit this, I would have been terrible at Operation K Street Thot.

I talk too much, or worse yet, I talk back. So in reality this combination of me, my Republican sugar daddy, and the people in the room longing for sweet antebellum's return would have ended in disaster. Someone would have said something casually racist, and I, full of wealthy people's whiskey, would have surely made a face that prompted an inquiry that gave way to a public shaming.

I'm pretty sure eventually a request for something sexual would have been made and promptly denied, resulting in my immediate firing.

I'm not sure I would have been compensated properly with all these strikes against me. That is, if anyone hired me at all. If anyone wanted to continue the situation in spite of such asterisks, I guarantee they would not want to pay my misandry tax, dismissing it as a personal problem.

However, even if I could be convinced to become more accommodating and try this hustle out, I'm too old now. One of my friends tried to convince me otherwise, citing some vintage thots we watch on basic cable. It was so sweet of her to tell me whoring is still an option, but as I explained to her, you become an aging gay by twenty-five. I'm . . . not twenty-five.

It may be too late for me, but if you're out there with a line of work that's more or less the City Girls catalog live, best wishes and private jet trips to you. You get no judgment from me.

BIG TOE HO

Did you know people with foot fetishes will pay you for pictures of your feet? Not to toe-suck-shame anyone, but when

I first found that out, I wanted to vomit in my mouth a little. However, I had Casamigos swirling in my mouth at the time of that reveal, so I stopped myself from wasting such a high grade of liquor in this economy.

There are so many people named Michael, but it took me more than thirty years to befriend another person named Michael who has managed to be far more inappropriate than me. He won't admit that, but it matters not. I finally have these bragging rights and I'm going to make the most of them.

A group of us was hanging out, and like many people of select generations who hang out in this decade, we were looking at Instagram instead of each other. That's when I saw the picture of some Instathot—that is to say, someone who posts nothing but thirst traps that I probably both judge and hit "like" on. He was showing his feet just swinging in the air. For foot freaks, this is apparently the equivalent of showing some ass. Through Michael, I learned that this was done as a means to elicit attention from those who would potentially pay to see more. I'm no Ronan Farrow, but I was tempted to perform some quick investigative journalism.

That is to say, I took another sip of my tequila and asked Michael, "What the fuck did you just say?"

Come to find out, a lot of you people in this world know about this. Some have even partaken in the practice to cover a few Sprint bills or weekend excursions to Miami or Dubai during one of those glitch sales. Well, ice y'all out.

The first dude I ever dated used to slightly mock me for my "pretty hands and pretty feet." Sadly, my feet aren't as pretty as they used to be. I don't know if it's from walking around New York so much or racism, but until I go through some intense pedicures and return to splendor, I can't make money from someone's fetish fund. But if you've maintained, you're welcome for this idea.

TEACHER

I got an email once from a recruiter for the Los Angeles Independent School District asking me if I had any interest in becoming a teacher. I received it several months after graduating from college, while working as a grossly underpaid freelance writer who kept up a hobby of job hunting. The recruiter saw my résumé on CareerBuilder and asked if we could speak on the phone to discuss an opportunity he felt I would be a good fit for. The opportunity in question would be me teaching English in high school.

Did I have any interest in teaching? I did not, but I was interested in full-time work. Getting out of Houston was always a good idea in my mind, and the idea of tipping west was becoming of greater interest, albeit for entirely different reasons than teaching. As someone around me at the time noted, at the age of twenty-four, taking a slight detour might not be the worst action to consider. Another spoke of it in terms of the potential impact.

There is a paucity of Black male teachers in U.S. schools, with them only representing 2 percent of the nation's educators, according to a report on racial diversity released from the Department of Education in 2016. I went to majority Black schools, but even in those settings, there were not many Black male teachers around. Of those few, two had a positive impact on me—unsurprisingly both were English teachers for me in high school.

The Black man who had the biggest impact on me, though, was Mr. Morris. He was a teacher's assistant when I was in elementary school. In elementary school, most of the adults around you feel old. Mr. Morris did not. He looked like he was in his twenties and felt cooler than the other adults around. Most of my teachers were encouraging, but he used to lavish me with praise differently. He used to point at me often and say, "Michael is going to be president."

It made me smile every single time. (I have never wanted to be president, but I have wanted to be a U.S. senator since high school. That is, before Mitch McConnell rendered the senate moot.) Because of memories like that, I was able to picture what a similar impact from me could look like. Most of all, I would be helping fill a massive, specific void.

As lovely as that sounds, absolutely not.

The only time I have envied a teacher's life is when Mr. Cooper sang the *Hangin' with Mr. Cooper* theme with En Vogue.

I find that I don't like a lot of children who are not related to me—and while this may end with a standoff in front of the cornbread dressing (not stuffing, mongrels) at whichever of the holidays I show up to at a later date, I really only mean my sister's kids and the spawn of select cousins. In my senior year of high school, one of my electives was the day care center we had on campus for the teen moms and low-income folks who couldn't afford child care. So, plenty of niggas over there.

We were taking care of children aged three to five. My aversion to children besides my nieces and certain second cousins aside, I was pretty good at watching the children because I am not a monster, I just talk like one sometimes. I read stories with eagerness and entertainment value. I helped them with their lil' assignments since this world has enough illiteracy in it. I was good at administering nap time because I wanted to talk about the Ashanti and Tweet debut albums without so much interference.

I didn't hate it, but those kids wore my ass out more often than not. And no, doing day care for toddlers isn't the same as teaching high school students, but uh, the former sounds like a much more enviable position to be in. I have been one of those students in a classroom led by a teacher who seemingly fell into teaching rather than answered a calling. You know the difference in how they speak to you, how they treat you, and how they run their classroom. The sacrifices they make are not ideal, but they speak to a greater purpose.

That's why teachers have my absolute respect. Who would any of us be without good teachers? However, if the aim for me was to leave a field (even if intended to be a temporary move, which sounds easier said than done once you go in an opposite direction) that presented a litany of challenges, such as proper compensation for my work and tangible support in making sure I do my best job imaginable, is working in the public school system the best alternative?

That's why I didn't take that job. I can be mad at home and save gas. Now, I do root for the rich to get taxed more fairly and for school funding and property taxation to get a divorce so the kind of schools I attended are allocated more resources. All of which would make teaching more appealing.

Please don't hate me, teachers. It's not y'all; it's the system. And it's some of those kids, but that's not your fault, either.

FALSE PROPHET

I am fascinated that Louis Farrakhan is still invited places. Not only has he had long acknowledged he "helped create the atmosphere" that led to Malcolm X's assassination, he has maintained archaic views about women and abhorrent ones about Jewish people and queer folk. Traditionally, helping facilitate a political leader's death while being a sexist, homophobic, anti-Semitic egomaniac sounds like the résumé of an incredibly successful conservative media personality, but Farrakhan is Black, so he doesn't get considered right wing. Please don't ask me about America's silly-ass metric of assessing one's political ideology with regards to the left-and-right binary. I didn't make the rules; the whites did.

No matter how horrific his views are, Farrakhan maintains a certain stature within the Black community. He gets invited to Aretha Franklin's funeral. He is asked to speak at Nipsey Hussle's memorial. If you are Black and famous enough to warrant a televised service, there is a high probability that Farrakhan will be in attendance, if not one of the main attractions. There are plenty of public figures who manage to skate by on past laurels and their overall legacy, but betcha by golly wow does this slick-haired man deserve bragging rights on such a feat. If you dare speak ill of him, plenty o' folks will defend him; not to say that your critiques are invalid, but that they should be overlooked like the slight dent on that fancy car that gets you pulled over in white neighborhoods.

It is remarkable.

I once saw Louis Farrakhan speak at Howard University. Not because I liked the nigga or anything. By the time the former calypso singer with the smooth conk rolled to campus, my mind had already been made up about him (see list of aforementioned offenses). A man like that isn't a riddle, but while I found him repugnant, I wanted to see the show for myself. And it was very much a show.

Farrakhan's humanity might get a bad review on Yelp from me, but he is a gifted orator. He also knows his audience. He knew most of the people in attendance weren't there to hear about Dr. Yakub, so he went for the target that keeps him in business: white supremacy. And when it wasn't about white supremacy, it was about *us*, although he took on the cadence of a speaker referred to as "the good reverend" rather than anyone I've heard from his actual religion. Again, he knows his audience. I get the many reasons he retains stature—legacy, oratorial gifts, and the like—but he has earned a higher level of hateration all the same.

However, in recent years, there is the odd association the Nation of Islam has with the Church of Scientology. I read about this years before Leah Remini rang the alarm about the Nation of Islam's becoming one of the Haus of Xenu's besties on an episode of her docu-series *Leah Remini: Scientology and the Aftermath*, but seeing former members call Farrakhan out on camera for selling out his flock to vanilla latte–colored liars should have been a bigger deal, no? Dianetics, L. Ron Hubbard, Xenu, Tom Cruise, and the rest of Marvin the Martian's clique don't have much in common with the NOI's ideology.

So how is Farrakhan able to sell both bean pies and spaceship tickets?

Bill Maher employs an acidic tone whenever bemoaning the caustic impact organized religion has had on society, but he does have a point that there are plenty of suckers roaming the Earth ready to be taken advantage of by someone under the guise of a spiritual awakening. It's not just the Honorable Minister Farrakhan. I was raised Catholic, and in the same way his terrible views about select groups are glossed over because he is believed to be speaking some larger truth, a similar verdict could be rendered about any given pope in my lifetime—yes, even including Pope Francis, who expresses similar outdated and offensive opinions about women's autonomy and queer and trans people's right to live as divinely designed, only he presents his regression in softer shapes and tones. When it comes to cooler, IG-ready holy scammers, while I can understand the urge to get on your knees with and/or for Carl Lentz, the Hillsong Church is not queer-friendly. Justin Bieber has bops, but his affiliation doesn't excuse the reputation his Australian-based church has rightly earned.

When I was presented with an offer to join the priesthood, I said no for a number of reasons, but largely I didn't pick up what that religion was putting down anymore. But what if I knew that I wasn't a believer and decided to spread the gospel for tax breaks anyway? I like the idea of getting famous enough where I am invited to speak at the funerals of various R&B and southern rap legends.

And so we are clear, if I were to change my mind, I would never, ever create a religion based on Beyoncé. Not only would that be predictable from me; it's also offensive to my lord and gyrator, who loves Jesus. She would also sue me for copyright infringement. Don't try and get me popped.

Let me paint a different picture: Me, in Saint Laurent distressed denim and tee (God likes this for me, I'm certain), speaking about the white man and, because I'd be hipper, the 53 percent of white women who voted for Donald Trump in the 2016 presidential election, while select works from Kelly Price's catalog play in the background? After that, I could give a testimonial about her deep cuts. (If you have never heard her song "Don't Say Goodbye," do yourself a favor and put that on loop—and where legally available, add some sativa to your listening session. You're welcome.) I already know what I would say at Bun B's homegoing, although I pray that scientists figure out how to make "UGK 4 Life" more than a slogan.

This might have sounded outlandish in a pre–Kanye West Presents Sunday Service world, but if Hip-Hop David Koresh can exploit a Black cultural tradition for self-gain, why not me? If he can get a choir to cover SWV's "Weak" for a crowd of majorly white people in the dustier parts of California, maybe I can up the ante by doing the same with Brownstone and S.I.S.T.A. covers? I could inspire with lies, and since I'm not an awful human being, you could enjoy me guilt free.

Doesn't that sound lovely? It does. And tax-free.

Gays in Atlanta allegedly like to run credit card scams, but that sounds like it's tempting fate with the feds. I'd rather annoy God a little bit by telling the masses we group chat. If God sends a lightning bolt my way, at least it'll be outside of a cell.

The only problem with this plan is that despite my heathenism, I have a heart. I'm not the kind of person that could start a religion to scam people desperate for a leader, no matter how vile or idiotic. I maintain a reverence for religion and the religious. Like a goddamn sucker who can't appreciate the blessing of living a tax-exempt existence. Lift me in prayer.

REPUBLICAN

There will always be a space for some member of some marginalized community to lend their minority status to an ideology that works to maintain the status quo. They say God doesn't make any mistakes, but the mediocre Negroes who lend their melanin to white supremacy's cause for self-gain are a direct challenge to that. I could name plenty of those types, but since they would enjoy that, no thank you.

I can say that while it doesn't apply to all Black conservatives, the following description applies to most of them.

Their hair often suggests that they haven't ventured to a Black barbershop or hair salon in at least a decade. They tend to repeat the same lines about Democrats being racists in the 1960s and how the party itself is one big plantation. They suddenly believe in the intellectual musings of Kanye West, Stacey Dash, and Diamond and Silk. They tend to feign victimhood, often. They can never attend an Essence Festival without fear of being shamed by various aunties spanning regions and accents.

I would rather die.

CORPORATE LAWYER

My communications law professor, who I believe worked for President Clinton, reminded me of Kyle Barker from *Living Single* if Kyle Barker had decided to be an attorney rather than a funds manager.

I think I told him this to his face once because I like to remind people what animated figures they best resemble or what TV character best describes their essence. He didn't appear to mind the practice because we had a good rapport. Much of that had to do with how I showed up to class. I had an internship at C-SPAN and, like a dummy, tried to dress way too nice for the unpaid labor. Side note: It wasn't until after I left the internship that I found out a potential sugar daddy had a thing for me, so that sugar baby thing could have really happened.

Anyhow, Professor Kyle Barker liked that I was dressed up and was into politics. So much so that he routinely called on me in class despite me not having my hand up because it was 6 p.m. and I was in a classroom for two hours. I didn't want to talk to anyone. I wanted to be at Alero on U Street drinking margaritas at happy hour. But he got me to talk because I didn't have much of a choice.

Near the end of the semester, he had a suggestion: law school. It was something to the effect of it spoke more to my potential than broadcast journalism. It reminded me of the time I was told during my first internship interview—for a position at a radio station—that I should have been interviewing at City Hall instead.

The summer going into my senior year of high school, I participated in my school's co-opt program. The program allowed high school seniors to spend half their days working at some professional outlet. My sister did it when she was in high school. I wanted to make money and was over working at amusement parks and movie theaters (well, for a day at the latter; I quit when I couldn't stomach the racism of the people at that particular location).

I was working at a Black-owned law firm in a bank building in the Galleria area. If you have an office in the Galleria area, you have money—especially back then. Kudos to these Negroes. A Black man founded the firm and his wife ran the office. The wife looked like Salli Richardson, whom I choose to describe as Angela from *A Low Down Dirty Shame*, although her IMDb page is very much full of current work, thank you so very much.

The job itself was fine, but I remember being mostly just interested in finding out that the firm represented certain members of Destiny's Child around the time of the breakup. Naturally, that is all I really cared about that entire summer.

I did my work as instructed, but much like me in a classroom, I was a social butterfly. Salli-esque did not enjoy this quality about me. In fact, she called me into her office once to effectively ask me to shut my goofy ass up and leave the associates alone. Unfortunately, they kept coming to me anyway. The white girl that had chic glasses that made her look like the baddie lawyers you see on broadcast dramas. Very into it. There was a Black dude named Rod. I remember Rod's name because Rod was incredibly joyous to look at.

He was very handsome, kept a nice fade at all times, and had a great body that he made sure you noticed by way of his shirt that was tight but not pathetically so. Same for the fit of his pants. Whew, he made denial hard. And he treated me like a little brother. I wish I remembered his last name. He was straight, but people change.

As a kid from Hiram Clarke working at a law firm with fancy Blacks, I suppose this could have theoretically altered my vision of my future, but I knew then this was not me. Again, all I cared about was Destiny's Child and running my mouth.

Lawyers like to argue; I do not. Lawyers talk about things like torts; I can talk to you about downloading torrents once upon a time, because I always forget what a tort is until I go to Google. I'm sure it'd be fine if I worked at a firm like the one on *Ally McBeal*. At least they had a bar downstairs and let you perform whenever the spirit called.

However, many lawyers do make a lot of money, so maybe that's what Professor Kyle Barker meant about my potential. And the more I think about it, he probably meant I should be more strategic about my media-related goals. There are plenty of lawyers on television blabbering about politics. You don't get paid for those appearances unless contracted to do so, but if you so happen to catch enough wave to earn a contract, that is more money on top of the money you're making as an attorney.

I will admit that I told myself if I didn't make certain inroads on some professional goals by the age of thirty, I'd take a frank assessment of my career and life and whether or not it was time to make a change to better situate both. One of the options would be to consider taking the LSAT and seeing how it goes.

I never went through with that, but in hindsight, maybe I should have considered this prospect when it was first presented to me. I would not have done criminal law because that's too much based on what I see on TV. I would only do corporate law since those lawyers seem the wealthiest on TV. And on Instagram. And on dates. And at parties.

Only problem with this plan is it would require more schooling, which means more debt, so unless I decide to write hood lit novels to cover the costs, no.

But stay tuned.

THIS IS A STORY ABOUT CONTROL

You have to shake the handle a little bit in order to completely quiet the toilet—or *commode*, depending on your level of country. If you don't, that thing will never stop making noise. Not an especially loud noise, but one that will grow to irritate you after a while. My mom has to remind me of this whenever I'm back at her house, which, in recent years, has been far less often.

She approached the closed door and repeated herself as I was washing my hands and face. Given she couldn't see me, she missed me rinsing off the remnants of the bigger problem that was happening behind the locked door.

"Michael, shake that handle so it can stop. Your dad still hasn't fixed it."

Within seconds, she got a "Yes, ma'am" and a corrective action. My penchant for being a creature of habit failed me in that respect, but the usual protocol for what had happened only a few moments prior had gone the same as it always did. I had turned on the faucet, letting both the hot and cold water flow to the point where they could drown out the noise of me shoving two fingers down my throat, forcing myself to purge.

I had learned over time to minimize the volume of my vomiting, to make certain that I would not be found out. That, coupled with some other tidbits I picked up along the way, was what helped me develop a bit of a system, a process.

You should drink a little something as you eat to help make it come back up easier, but not too much, lest it get messy and feel even more wretched than it already does. If your throat is too dry and you force yourself too hard, you may end up hurting yourself. Well, I suppose you're already hurting yourself doing this, but you don't want to make this any more painful than it needs to be.

I always wondered if my mom could hear me whenever I'd sneak into the bathroom, lock the door, and spend a few minutes longer than felt usual inside. To this day, she has never said anything to me directly about it. A part of me thinks she suspected it was happening because, in spite of my belief that I never quite deserved the reputation of being the "sneaky" child, I've never been a good liar. Nor was it exactly a secret that I was uncomfortable with my weight. And, of course, I would often go into the bathroom not long after I had eaten something.

I was never sure who else in the house heard me, either. Boys spend too much time in the bathroom for a number of reasons. I could have been releasing anything, and yeah, I didn't blame them for not wanting to think about just *what* was being released.

Toward the end of fifth grade, my appetite started to increase. That's normal for any growing child, much less a boy inching toward his teenage years and all of the hormones that arrive with them. But in my case, this involved graduating from a Happy Meal to a Six-Piece Nugget Meal. And then a Nine-

Piece Nugget Meal. A few times, I asked for a twenty-piece Nugget order all for myself.

Once, as my mother drove my brother and me down West Fuqua toward the McDonald's located on Almeda Road in Houston—right across the street from the railroad tracks—I made the first request for a twenty-piece. I said it with such urgency, too. I could make out the surprise in my mom's response. After the Nuggets, soon came my request for a Quarter Pounder with Cheese Meal (no pickles, no onions) supersized with a Coke. By middle school, it was a Double Quarter Pounder with Cheese, also with no pickles and onions. Until adulthood, I could not wrap my brain around crunchy-ass onions with a burger. Instead, I got onion *rings* on a burger. See, I was from the land of fried cheesecake, fried Oreos, and maybe even fried grape Gatorade if you find the right fool willing to perfect the recipe.

The higher calorie intake I was enjoying might not have been so bad if I had still been an active kid. Instead, I stopped moving around so much. The toll of growing up in that house and seeing my father's alcoholism and anger be taken out on my mom first and foremost, and by extension the rest of us, made me sad, made me feel powerless, and made me angry. Between this and having to meet new people at a new school with my increasing weight, I leaned toward isolation. I was reading more, and I watched a lot of television, but I also took to the internet because it was a way for me to start exploring some feelings about boys that I was told were unnatural and unbecoming. I may have been fat, but the thing I quickly learned about the internet was you could pretend to be someone different in order to talk to people in a profoundly honest way.

My dad used to always say, "I like your size." I didn't believe that nigga whenever he said it, but I loved him for that. I may have found him to be a monster more times than not, but I took this as his way of trying to reassure his chubby son about his rising weight and stagnant height, as other kids around the neighborhood were leaning out and rapidly growing taller. My mom noticed the weight gain as well, but never said anything directly about it. One time, though, I finished playing outside and walked back into the house, and she told me to go back outside and "run a little more."

In hindsight, she may have simply wanted a bit of peace. Between working on her feet all day as a registered nurse, being married to a man who often drove her insane with his drunken tirades, and being saddled with taking care of three children, for her it was one of the few times the house was quiet. But this is probably being very generous—'cause really, to this day, I still hear her "run a little more" comment as telling me to sweat out the Sweet and Sour Sauce she procured for the three thousand Chicken Nuggets I was consuming.

In elementary school, with my buck teeth, complexion, and slim frame, I looked like Alvin Seville. By the start of middle school, I looked like his chubbier brother Theodore. When I got glasses, I looked like Simon if he ate Alvin and parts of Theodore (the dark meat).

Having said that, I can't say that I was routinely picked on. I'm sociable when I want to be, so I had a lot of friends. However, many teens can't help but act like the highest grade of asshole, and some classmates couldn't resist talking about my weight, presumably feeling it too great a target to miss.

In honors biology, a boy I had the biggest crush on likened me to the Pillsbury Doughboy and literally poked me in the stomach with a grin; he waited for me to mimic the laugh from the old commercials. I should have bit him (and not in the fun, sexual way). That would not be the last time he did it. Others, notably those who were not my friend and/or were pissed at me, were far harsher, engaging the subject matter as a means to hurt my feelings and shut me up.

Unbeknownst to them, I never needed anyone else's assistance in order to feel bad about my body. I saw the other boys in class. The ones I had crushes on that I couldn't reveal. I saw the men in magazines, on television shows, and wherever else fit men gleamed. I knew I didn't look like any of them. I understood being 180 pounds in the seventh grade was not ideal. Nor were the man boobs forming on my chest around the same time as the girls around me were maturing.

But in keeping with the mantra "Don't come for me unless I send for you," the thing about growing up in a violent home helmed by two people who know how to *cut* deep is that you know how to cut people down to size when pushed. Cut them down so much that they either shut up or want to run up. If the latter happened, all that did was allow me a means to channel the burgeoning rage that defined my chaotic home life. But tit-for-tats don't take away the burden of tits sitting on your chest and your feeling hopeless about it.

Still, this was before I began to make myself throw up.

I started thinning out in high school. I was still on the chubbier side my freshman year, but the summer going into my sophomore year, I grew significantly taller and, as a result, started to get leaner in my appearance. My mom will chop you down to size, but she's an itty-bitty thing. My dad ain't but that much taller; he has the face of Katt Williams but the demeanor of T.I.—i.e., he is basically Scrappy-Doo, with a smaller frame but ready to wreak havoc. (He has the felonies to prove it.) Thankfully, my dad is an anomaly on his side, so while the Arceneaux gene pool comes with twists and turns, at least height is widespread.

With that kicking in, though my body wasn't perfect, I was able to fit into medium-sized shirts again.

Bitch.

Do you know what it's like to be a chubby-ass kid in junior high—where our worst impulses go to vacation—and suddenly be able to fit in a medium? After being extra large. After wearing a larger denim size than your dad. After jiggling to a song that asks you for jiggling, but not in the way your body was doing it? It felt like a miracle.

But miracles can fade.

I always say I wish I had run track in high school. For starters, there were a bunch of fine dudes on our track team. Some uppity niggas in Houston might have talked shit about my hood-ass high school, but beyond many a brilliant Negro attending school there was the fact that in terms of the genre of Black bae, the hood is a bountiful land of snacks. And track guys have the best bodies. Before I got fat, I had been an athletic-ish kid. I definitely enjoyed running. As a Madison High School student and Hiram Clarke native, it's not like I hadn't had to sprint running from niggas shooting before. Ugh, I would have been perfect for the track team for a variety of reasons, but my goofy ass just didn't do it.

Not working out and at the same time eating poorly will catch up with anyone, even if your metabolism is at Avengers-level as a teen. In the morning, I had my best friend Kim buy me an extreme sausage sandwich, no egg—every single morning. Why was it extreme? Because it was two pork sausage patties stacked on each other with American cheese, between a bun that would have been more apt for a burger. It was glorious, but why was I eating such a thing in the a.m.? For lunch, it was fried chicken strips or some other fast food that my friends would sneak out to get. Sneak out, ha; we were too monitored for that. By sneak out, I mean they were let out of the parking garage by security, who looked the other way if they brought them something back. I did not have a car, so I could not sneak out any damn where.

After school let out and I made it back home, my dad, who in an effort to appease us for whatever trauma he had caused his children the night before, would get me whatever I wanted from Jack in the Box. And what I always got was the following order: a Bacon Ultimate Cheeseburger (an Ultimate offers two burger patties) with curly fries, jumbo-sized with a strawberry soda and two tacos. Those two tacos were fried.

By senior year, those bad eating habits, coupled with my lack of joining the track team, had resulted in my weight ballooning. That's when I started trying to make myself throw up. I didn't want to go back to fat. I didn't like the way I looked or felt before I got slimmer. All I could think about was not so much the taunts of others, but the self-criticism I gave myself over how my body looked.

In college, I lost weight because I was struggling with adjusting to life at Howard University, fighting myself over the reality that I was gay, and as a result of that and the depression I had packed with me from Houston, not eating a whole lot. I also walked everywhere, which I never had to do in Houston because who does much of that in hot-ass Texas? I wasn't purging as much, but it still happened from time to time.

I've never been quite sure whether or not I would say I

was bulimic. My purging has consistently taken place through the years, but it was never done on a consistent basis. I never quite committed to it in that way. I ultimately learned to eat healthier and exercise regularly. I always knew there were better ways to go about addressing my weight issues, but I didn't bother for far too long.

The most fit I have ever been was around the time I turned thirty. I was doing much better after initially relocating to New York, so I eventually got the nerve to work with a trainer. She was a teensy-tiny little thing, but she was a lesbian who looked as if the Shirley Wilson character from *What's Happening!!* were several inches shorter and did body lifting. I find that to be a compliment because let the record state she also had a tighter fade and better wardrobe. She was fun, but gave me reasons to be concerned about her. She would offer me tequila mixed in with her sports drink during my workouts. Likewise, she asked if I wanted to smoke weed with her afterward. She was looking for a friend, but even if she was well-meaning, she was crazy in a way that was part ha-ha and part . . . whatever way leads to violence. To wit, she went off on her manager, which is how she got fired—not just from there but from the gym across the street that she tried to get me to join after that.

Whatever, she was a great trainer. Because she behaved like a lot of the awful, overcompensating straight Black men driving everyone else insane, she had me doing exercises that made even the hurly-burly meatheads in the gym looking in awe. Some of them applauded me after we wrapped. It's unclear if it was before or after their injection of steroids, but I digress. I stopped working out with her not because she scared me sometimes, but because those freelance checks that were pouring in dried up and whatever little bit was coming in had to go to rent and my loans.

This financial frustration caused me to return to some old habits.

If you had told me I was an emotional eater a couple of years ago, I might have told your happy ass to shut up and stop projecting. But in trying to better understand myself and my issues in every facet of my life, I started to examine my relationship with food. How I would not eat during some dark moments, but in another extreme, teeter toward gluttony in order to deal with some other emotion. That proved manageable, though not an ideal way to live.

I learned to eat healthier foods, and when I wanted to deviate from them while reckoning with a perceived crisis, I explored acceptable alternatives instead of previous vices. What remained a struggle was coming to accept that I was someone prone to emotional purging. By then, I knew if I wanted a better body, I needed to work out and eat right. I saw that I didn't need to purge in order to attain some perceived goal. So I stopped. I really did stop. Until I didn't.

Whenever I feel not in control, especially when it comes to money, I panic. I overanalyze. I over-criticize myself. I sink into a state of mind that coerces me into questioning everything about myself. The purging was no longer about my weight, but about the desire to feel as if I was in control of some aspect of my life. No matter how inane, self-destructive, irrational, flat-out idiotic that line of thinking was, it's where my head was. It never panned out that way in practice, but it was a habit all the same.

As had been the case in the past, it wasn't necessarily a daily occurrence, but it was growing more frequent and beginning to mirror my younger years, when I had taken to that action the most. At the same time, maybe I had been kidding myself all along. Did it really matter if I didn't do it daily if I would still do things like excuse myself to the bathroom at a restaurant with friends in order to go throw up everything I had just eaten?

There's no magic trick to stop doing it. In my case, I simply recognized that this was a habit that needed to be managed and stopped. Plus, there was a part of me that found it not just stupid of me, but wasteful.

As much as I cherish my beloved Pappadeaux, those hoes have always been expensive and the prices have only climbed steeper with time. So when I fly back to Houston and go eat at the spot I consider to be my cuisine Mecca, am I going to keep throwing up $20 worth of fried alligator? In this economy? With my debt? Who do I think I am? Is this what every Black parent meant when asking, "You got McDonald's money?" Come to think of it, my mom doesn't read my books, but should she stumble upon the tidbit that I might have thrown up even fourteen of those four thousand Nuggets she purchased for me over the years (to be fair to McDonald's, they had mad coupons back then), she might ask for restitution. (Okay, she won't, but I should not be wasting money.) That includes all of the chicken wings I craved and later disrespected by not fully digesting them.

I'm sorry to all, especially the drums, which I happen to like more than flats, but I eat both as a true believer in chicken.

In all sincerity, I have not been miraculously healed from the bad practice. Rather, I am proactive about not succumbing to it. Yes, for practical reasons that extend beyond the financial. Maybe one day I can get another trainer to attain a certain body type, but in the meanwhile, I can trust myself enough to have the discipline to get to the gym, no matter how late the start feels. I cringe at using verbiage that borders on saccharine, but on a fundamental level, there has to be a greater love of self that supersedes setbacks, and the dangerous coping mechanisms we turn to in order to deal.

Worries about overwhelming debt will not be curbed with induced vomiting. There are other ways to deal. But this isn't just about dealing with disappointment. I had to not just understand, but embrace the truth that each time I purged, I was abusing myself. Hardship and whatever moments of doubt that arrive don't warrant such self-sabotage. I've written so much about the damage other people have done to me. It's time to admit more of the things I've done to myself.

It's not just for the sake of transparency. I do not owe anyone this information. Still and all, keeping secrets like this are about maintaining control. I just want to be free.

NEVER HAVE I EVER

He was there to use his mouth, not his words.

After I had encountered bed bugs and Megyn Kelly enthusiasts during comically terrible attempts at having some fun-filled fornication, I accepted that I was never going to become a great ho. The cruelty of defeat notwithstanding, I refused to believe that I could not, at the very least, become a semi-decent one.

Aaliyah sang, "If at first you don't succeed, you can dust it off and try again." It's such a good line to draw inspiration from and body roll to. In this moment, this was me dusting my dick off and trying again. (Rest in peace, Baby Girl.)

Such efforts did not require conversation, however, and most assuredly not one centered on my romantic failures, real or perceived. But after he finished, he felt compelled to inquire more about me. Me, a stranger about whom the only real knowledge he had was how I tasted. He was clearly violating the golden rule: *When it's all over, please get up and leave.*

I suppose he was, uh, impressed, or um, at least had enjoyed himself, because after he rose and sat on my bed, he jested that he felt sorry for my former boyfriends. That would have been much cuter if he had said it while putting his shoes back on and vacating the premises. Unfortunately, it would take longer for that to happen, so in the meantime I quickly corrected him and revealed that I'd never had one of those. That's when his curiosities piqued again, albeit for reasons that were no longer prurient in nature.

Why hadn't I just smiled and nodded when he said that? He had actually looked at his shoes as if he were finally ready to put them back on and get the hell out of my tiny little apartment. He was almost gone! Now I was subjected to an impromptu interrogation from a person I had, as of three minutes ago, planned never to speak to again.

Judgment from a jump-off. How fun! So much fun I could leap into traffic holding a sign reading "End it already, Jesus!"

None of the detailed questions he asked were any of his business. *What's the longest time you've dated someone? Or have you never dated anyone at length? If so, why not? If you have, why didn't it work out, and by work out, I mean, did you use the terms "boyfriend" and "relationship"?*

Some people might have been flattered by this impromptu demand for an in-depth interview, but as someone who has done interviews and has been interviewed, I think that timing and purpose matter. This prime-time interview request served me no purpose. Why did he care, anyway?

I did not flat-out ask, *Why are you still here, playboy?* but my face presumably conveyed as much, as did my curt responses to each of his questions. I then picked up my remote control, and this pivot begot a shift to bitchiness from him. I would have felt bad about this, but it was the fastest way to get him and his curiosities out of the door and furthest from my mind now that the assigned task was completed.

Ariana Grande, or "Ponytail," as I prefer to call her (affectionately so), was already a thing, but sadly, "thank u, next" hadn't been released when this went down. Had it been, perhaps I could have started singing a revised version where I thanked him for his fucking mouth and sent him on his way.

Thank you for your services. Feel free to never, ever bother me again. Thanks, again.

I assumed that I would never see him again, but since God likes to troll, I did eventually see him at my gym. In fact, I started to see him every other day for a couple of months or so. We never spoke. I ignored him completely, sans the one time we made eye contact and gave each other the same gesture meaning that future conversations were not necessary or encouraged. All was well that ended well.

However, I didn't forget the last comment he had made to me. That he felt "sorry" for me. This was in response to the revelation that I had not been in a committed relationship this deeply into adulthood. I was in my thirties. I had friends who were married, divorced, and remarried. I had friends with kids or who were planning to have them soon. Outside of one sole couple, though, most of them were straight. There were some spare lesbians with kids that I am including in this bunch, but all of them had come from past relationships with men.

He was echoing the concerns I'd heard from others around me—his real offense that sparked my less-than-gracious reaction. I will concede that maybe it leaned on rude—and that it gave way to his slick talk. Even jump-offs don't want you to be alone, y'all.

By the time he said what he said, I was already hearing it

from friends of all orientations. Maybe not so plainly and not done in an attempt to shame me, but yeah, I knew what others made of the fact that I hadn't been in a long-term relationship. They all meant well. They didn't want to think of me dying alone one day because I tripped over trying to rub Bengay on my knees after dancing too hard to Megan Thee Stallion. (For the record, I don't want that, either, even if it sounds as if I would go out doing what I loved.)

And also for the record, it wasn't as if I had purposely avoided ever having a boyfriend.

In my defense, queer people have to deal with the reality that our straight counterparts have experiences in their teens and twenties that many of us don't get to have until much later in life. We have to learn how to date; formulate what we think we like; after trial and error, figure out what we really need and then go pursue that.

Some blessed individuals come out and immediately find themselves a boo. And then another one. And then another one. And then a husband. And then they and the husband stick together but become open. Actually, they were probably open before they got married, but have since made addendums to that arrangement to avoid a conclusion that ends with a division of assets. That's not my business unless they send an invitation, but I digress.

That's amazing for all of those people who find love in this hopeless place. Really, round of applause (shawty make that ass clap) for them.

But the rest of us don't necessarily follow a journey that features the same steps. Like, I date men. Men even know how horrible men are. Where is the compassion for my struggle?

When you really break it down, straight people start dating

in their teens, whereas I didn't really date the individuals I was attracted to until my twenties. So my thirties and a straight person's thirties aren't totally comparable.

If anything, I shouldn't be shamed until I'm at least forty-five. Then people can say, *Wow, what a weirdo you are.* Isn't that a fair courtesy to consider?

But since accountability is the move, I will acknowledge that it is my fault that I settled for "fake boyfriends" and "situationships" in the past. It is my fault for spending a lot of my time ducking emotional and physical intimacy. It is also my fault that after I made the choice to change my ways, I found new reasons to stifle myself.

No reason was more dominant than my willful decision to assume that my financial situation made me a less desirable partner—to the point where I truly started to believe that.

No one held me to any specific standard. I was judging myself by the standards I had set for myself. And the more I felt like I was behind on meeting them, the further removed I felt from getting close to anyone in a way that would lead to a relationship that would require even more of my energy. I would hate to have to feel like I couldn't hold my weight because I was sinking under the weight of my debt.

As dumb as this sounds—and I'm fine with that—I took one of those BuzzFeed polls that millions of us take in order to make the most of our procrastination. The quiz in question was designed to measure how dateable you are based on your order at the Cheesecake Factory. Let this quiz tell it: I was only 5 percent dateable based on my choices. That result was quite "nasty," as that sociopathic racist thot white folks made the 45th President of the United States of America would say.

But the text underneath provided the true cackle: "You're

not too dateable, at least not right now, and that's totally ok! You're focused on living your best life right now, which is pretty awesome. All good things come to those who wait, so just go on and wait a while."

It sounds better if you say you're trying to live life like that Jill Scott chorus so in the meantime your love life is that great Janet Jackson single from *Control* on loop. Better as in less obvious. So you don't admit to yourself that a BuzzFeed quiz read you for filth since somehow wanting to order a dulce de leche cheesecake and some spicy pasta dish was a gateway into your soul and your innermost doubts and fears.

I have tried not to let this form of pity—woo, woo, woo, you ain't got no boo—make me feel pitiful, but I estimate that I act human at least 70 percent of the time, so it gets to me at times. I didn't take kind to ole boy's unsolicited hypotheses about what was "wrong" with me because it arrived at a moment in which I had started getting it from others around me and was due to hear it with greater frequency.

You know, 'cause I was getting older and my relationship status remained stagnant.

You're thirty-one, and you've never had a boyfriend?

You're thirty-two, and you've never had a boyfriend?

You're thirty-three, and you've never had a boyfriend?

Nigga, you're thirty-four and you've never had a boyfriend?

And now you are thirty-five and you've never had a boyfriend?

My friend Chris reminded me that it isn't fair for me to judge myself by a standard that did not have me in mind when formulated.

I have long learned that if you give most functioning adults the opportunity to discuss relationships, they will skedaddle there at lightning speed. It's why I keep seeing those same debates about ass eating and $200 dates on Twitter and why I can't escape all 14 billion of those memes from people who despise being single on Instagram. They do both on Facebook several weeks after the other two social media platforms weigh in, obviously. It's mostly straight people leading the caravan, but with greater queer visibility comes the mirroring of select straight habits—never mind whether or not they're necessary.

"I think about this often," Chris said. "These benchmarks that Black gays have to create since we don't (or shouldn't) follow hetero milestones." We were talking about the myriad of ways Black queer people can find themselves alone, and eventually, embattled in loneliness. And he knew just what to say to make me feel better.

"I do think there's something to be said about making it to thirty-five and having your shit together, somewhat, without a man on your arm."

Together-ish is more like it, but we love friends who grade on a curve for the sake of our psyches. I thanked him for saying that before adding it could be worse; I could have made anyone a boyfriend for the sake of saying I had one.

I have had many friends who entered relationships because they were tired of not being in one. Some have admitted it outright; others pretend otherwise even if the good times in their respective relationships were about as long as this sentence. Of those, most went right back out to claim another, to similarly disastrous results. A few learned to slow the pace and let the right person find them. They all were, and are, trying. I've been trying, too, only with different results.

I decided to stop feeling bad about it upon the realization that there was nothing to feel so down about. I may not have had a boyfriend by name, but to many, that didn't suggest a failure in me. It was not as if I were walking around totally clueless and chaste.

I know what it's like to be in love; I know what it's like to waste time, money, and energy on someone who doesn't deserve it. I know what it's like to experience intimacy in all its shapes and sounds. I know that in time, when it's meant for something like that to happen in my life, it will.

What I know most is, time was not on my side by virtue of conditions beyond my control. How I reacted to them may have arguably prolonged what may or may not have been the inevitable, but ultimately a fixation on my stunted development—as a gay man and a millennial with debt—only extends it. Accepting this didn't miraculously alter my situation, but it did provide some long overdue acceptance of it. That and the reminder that things can always change.

As fate would have it, Grindr, the place that brought that man who brought those bedbugs into my apartment once, briefly allowed me the opportunity to be an advice columnist. In a column called "Dearly Beloved," a nod to both Prince and Iyanla Vanzant, I responded to people who wrote from countries all over the world.

An overwhelming number of the emails received were centered on the fear of being alone. Of those, a significant portion came from the perspective that for whatever reason, the writer had waited too long to date and was now convinced that they might never have a chance to post a boyfriend on social media. I deserve a Pulitzer for the number of different ways I came up with ways to articulate "You need to chill, ho."

Of those, by far the most read of the column was "Dearly Beloved, It's Never Too Late to Get Boo'd Up or Thot It Out." I found out from the editor in chief that it was the most read story on the site that year. I found this out about a week after Grindr abruptly shut the successful new outlet down. See why I worry about a boo before getting TV money?

In any case, here is what this person wrote:

> *I'm lonely in a way that a friend just can't help, okay. Main problem though?*
>
> *I haven't dated not once in my entire life. I have zero romantic or sexual experience. Absolutely. Zero. I feel like a newborn babe thinking I can play with wolves and I am TERRIFIED.*
>
> *So what am I to do? I am legit baffled by this whole thing and, considering my age, it's a little embarrassing and makes me not want to tell anyone my business or even go out there in the first place. Any advice?*

He was turning thirty and felt terrified over how he might sound to those more experienced than him.

And I said:

> *Will some people freak out? Perhaps. The same goes for a person potentially making you feel even more embarrassed about your lack of dating history and sexual experiences. I know that feeling; it can be humiliating. It can make you question why you even bothered. It may compel you to fall back into your cocoon. Please, don't let anyone do that to you. This also applies to dealing with a person who turns out to be the*

wrong one for you. Rejection hurts; it is self-sabotaging to cling to it.

Your past trauma and struggles may have shaped you, and in this case, delayed certain aspects of your life. Still, they do not define you. Nor do they have to deter you from your present choice to put yourself out there—which may yield you a more complete future. And once you meet the right person and forge a connection, those bad experiences will matter even less.

Yet, you will never learn any of this if you don't act and move forward. You may feel like a newborn baby now, but you won't feel that way for much longer. Some things come naturally for some, but for others, it takes much longer. Regardless, we all move on our time.

What you will have to do in the meantime is remain committed, know that you are worthy, and believe no matter how long it takes, you will find what you are looking for. So, when it comes to the question "What am I to do?" the answer is easy: try.

I don't know if he ever went back to check for my advice much less acted on it, but I meant every word. So much so that in the moments where the fear has crept back in, I have returned to my own words in order to make sure that I, too, remember that we cannot change what's happened, only how we choose to move afterward. You cannot allow yourself to be consumed by the standards set by others or any misguided reaction to the knowledge that everyone's journey is different.

You can have what you want—eventually, somehow. For me, that includes that wedding I wrote about having. I might even have a second one since statistically, I may end up with a conscious uncoupling.

In the meantime, all any of us can do is to keep trying. Some of you could learn to shut up while we do. Or at least make yourselves useful. If so many people were really concerned about me being single, they would have introduced me to Frank Ocean by now.

COGNAC AND CELEXA

After puberty deprived me of the chance to become the next Usher or at least a shorter sequel to Montell Jordan, I wish I had made a backup plan. Something along the lines of coming up with the genius idea to just make noises that sound like singing—preferably over a trap beat. Like Jeremih, a sort-of singer but undoubtedly a prophet and visionary. That should have been me repeating "don't tell 'em" for a little over four minutes. I don't have a doubt in my mind that YG and I wouldn't have ended up besties, blood.

Alas, I was blind for so long, but now I see there can be life outside of songs sung in the correct key. I don't have to be Trey Songz before he linked with a personal trainer or Usher any period prior to him acting like that uncle in the club you wish would accept his age in life and stop trying to prove he's still got it. I could be a rapper! Those two along with pretty much an entire generation of R&B artists record, behave, and present like most mainstream rappers anyway.

93

DO YOU KNOW HOW MUCH MONEY I COULD
MAKE AS A RAPPER?

Well, assuming I didn't get a 360 deal and secured endorse-
ments and a regular touring schedule. Maybe a docu-series exploring my life as the first lit gay rapper. You know, because
the mixtape is just the first step: kind of like a book is often
employed to make real money elsewhere. No shade.

I'm surprised I didn't consider this sooner. It's not like
my background wasn't surrounded by those who only thought
one of the three Bs could get them out of the hood: balls,
bricks, or bars. I was told to look away and focus on a bachelor's degree. I should have been working on my freestyles
instead.

Unfortunately, real niggas like me are not always supported
when it comes to a new dream born from epiphany—a dream
that is not nearly as implausible as it sounds on its surface,
thank you very much.

Sadly, when I told my friends that I wanted to be a rapper,
the shade started early.

I expect to be trolled by many of my friends, but friends you
hold near and dear to your heart should be the first to try and
get a feature now before your rate is too expensive. But no. Some
people don't know how to say yes to a less than ideal candidate
who true enough may not be your first, second, or even third
choice for the role they seek but is a much better alternative to
the other options available to you—thus, you might as well go
with the one that won't take as many years off of your life (if
not annihilate your entire existence through a cocktail of gross
incompetence fueled possibly by dementia though certainly by
utter stupidity along with general love for malfeasance).

I write that to say, Hillary Rodham Clinton, I understand,

sis, and if it's anything, I never gave a good goddamn about your emails.

My friend La is the first offender, as she said the meanest thing in response to my big reveal that I wanted to be a rapper and needed to figure out how to get studio time outside of following that strange shirtless man holding a sign promising studio time for the low low price of $20 per hour.

"You're too smart to be a rapper" is what she had the nerve to say in response. I sat there, in my raggedy office chair that I've refused to replace because it remains functional, and looked at my iPhone in disbelief. Thank God she hadn't written that from an Android. The diss in green text would have been even more insulting.

La is such a remarkable person of nuance, but in that moment, she treated me as if I were the charming, dusty but obviously handsome bus driver that gets scowled at by a mean, high-wage-earning light-skinned Black woman in a Tyler Perry production about a high saddity Negro wench that needs to be humbled by God and blue collar dick.

Too smart to be a rapper?

I beg your pardon, my high yella homie for life.

We have spoken of some rappers with intellect before, so I know she didn't mean it as if all rappers are dumb.

She was saying that I am too smart a person to be the ignorant rapper she knows I would want to be. Not as bad, but displeasing to hear all the same. It's a stance lacking in faith. Faith in me and my foolery potential. I don't remember what the Bible says about not encouraging your friend's rap dreams, but based on what I recall from catechism and Kirk Franklin's speaking parts on his songs, all those men claiming to ghostwrite for God would have deemed La very uncool in that moment.

I am an ignorant motherfucker. She knows this. But to her credit, I suppose one could describe me as a bit of an egghead, hardened by my upbringing in a rough environment. I choose to remain offended all the same. I believe it's important that friends see all sides of their friends, or more pointedly, whatever side benefits their friends at a given moment. More than anything, you can't tell an ignorant motherfucker like me they have too much sense to be a rapper. It stings.

Sadly, she wasn't the only friend who told me to hang it up before I set up my SoundCloud account.

I met my friend Sarah the second semester of my freshman year at Howard University. We became closer friends over time and forged a bond over activities such as twerking to Project Pat in Georgetown without worries or concerns about the white gaze. We have since matured in our thirties. We now do classier activities, such as seeing the stage play version of *Set It Off*, the the 1996 cult-classic film directed by F. Gary Gray that starred Queen Latifah, Jada Pinkett, Vivica A. Fox, and Kimberly Elise. I've never seen something so terrible yet delightfully entertaining. I'm sure that we smoked weed and had the highfalutin version of the chicken wings with mumbo sauce we ordered at the Hamilton in Washington, D.C., before the show. (Yes, this constitutes a ringing endorsement.)

Sarah has always been supportive of me and all of my ambitious plans. Even back in college, she consistently told me that I was going to enjoy great success in life. I came to learn that she didn't mean that in everything.

Sarah: Michael. Please. If any other profession was for you it would be video ho.

Me: I am flattered that you hold me in as high regard as Esther
Baxter in the "Freek-A-Leek" video.

Sarah: Yep! You wouldn't be a random Omarion video girl.

Assuaging my ego by leaning into praise of my aesthetic and
limberness is a shrewd way of delivering a harsh truth in sweet-
ish tones, but the hurt lingers on. When two people bond over
catfish and DJ Paul productions, that bond is sacred. So sacred
that I should be believed to have the ability to spit hot fire
rather than merely move my ass like it's inflamed.

I don't understand why my folks don't want better for me. It's
not as if I have to be musically talented to be successful in the
music industry. Consider that both as a compliment to technol-
ogy and an indictment of the lack of funding of art programs in
public schools. (VH1 tried to warn y'all with Save the Music.)
There are so many different routes for me to take with rap.

Some are more plausible than others.

One of my proudest moments in my work as indentured literary servant for multiple media outlets with varied levels of
capital in the role of an opinions dispenser was writing television recaps of *Love & Hip Hop*—specifically *Love & Hip Hop:
Atlanta*.

During that moment when television recaps—on reality shows, for sure—were enjoying peak online consumption,
there were many talented people offering some of the finest
humor writing for pennies on the dollar as they chronicled the
contemporary human conundrum that is being paid to argue
with a relative stranger a television producer has convinced you

is out to get you. The recaps that garnered the most attention on mainstream outlets were ones featuring predominately rich white cast members. I don't want to say I deserved at least a shout-out on Story Insta every Juneteenth, because it's not like I was a columnist for the *North Star,* but it was an artful contribution all the same.

The production team behind the show thought so anyway.

One day, I'll tell whatever youths are near me to gather around and go to YouTube in order to see the infamous *Love & Hip Hop: Atlanta* reunion featuring Joseline Hernandez and Stevie J—fueled by rage and whatever else left to speculation, bringing chaos to the reunion stage—with Joseline in particular going out of her way to fight every single person that ever said something slick about her while standing in front of a green screen. I'll tell them that I was there that day, and minutes before it all popped off, production team members were coming to meet me to say hello and thank me for recapping the show the way the other shows did on mainstream outlets (the team was majorly white before anyone makes an assumption).

I started to run into the people highest up that totem pole at other events. One of them, very high up, was once at the same premiere as me. They came over to say hello and asked how I had been, telling me they still kept up on my writing. I then found out why *Love & Hip Hop: Houston* was effectively shut down (gun control is necessary not solely for our safety, but also for the television spinoffs we crave). After hearing the specifics and going, "Yeah, that sounds like Houston," I mentioned buying a few of the new singles from select *Love & Hip Hop* cast members.

"Wait, you really buy those?"

They were shocked.

Some of the cast members of *Love & Hip Hop* have genuine talent. Others are more or less becoming novelty acts with very little pretense about possessing any discernible musical skill set, but with the hope that they can at least boost their club appearance fees with music that can be streamed.

Momma Dee, rapper Lil' Scrappy's mom, is a former pimp and nurse turned reality star who first dabbled in singing with "I Deserve." I adore her, and the song was catchy, but the vocals weren't there, and sadly, the "Anita Faker" market is grossly limited in its reach. Ever the hustler, however, Momma Dee released a dance song, "In That Order" featuring Yung Joc, a rapper who used to have hits before becoming a hair model on VH1 reality shows. I love Black people almost as much as Black people love a line dance. I bought the single because it was surprisingly catchy and I appreciated Momma's energy levels in the video, considering she's a grandmother who one presumes has been shot at a few times in her past and all.

I love Karlie Redd's "Louie Prada Gucci." The song was never officially released, but I ripped it from her SoundCloud and put it on my phone with my own main image so it's fine. I don't know if I would classify her as a singer, but she's not a rapper. She's like the vessel for the Auto-Tune who is a multi-hybrid talent. She, too, has no business in music, but a bop is a bop.

There have been gay rappers featured on the show, but most of their coverage has been centered on fighting, coming out, and fighting. I love us for real, but focus on the point of the show. Or not.

Some of the artists from the show are better than you would expect. Cyn Santana is best known for dating *Love & Hip Hop* star Erica Mena, who can't sing worth a damn, and Joe Budden, who can rap well but now makes money as a podcaster and television personality (in spite of past allegations of physically abusing women, no less), but her single was somewhat surprisingly impressive. To me, that means all you have to do is have sex with two types of artists—one with marginal at best ability and one with exceptional skills—and then combine the parts of their soul you sucked out of them, to make your own studio sessions go swimmingly. Maybe I should have sex with Lil' Fizz and then Drake before I hit the booth?

I want to do a song with Cyn Santana.

There is something inspiring about people who many might argue have no business in music going ahead and creating bops, but I don't want to be novelty, so of this genre of entertainer I'm more along the lines of K. Michelle and Lyrica Anderson, in that I socialize with the crazy and dabble in it myself from time to time, for a Mona Scott-Young check, but overall my music is taken seriously, even if I am not always to be taken seriously myself.

Another option for my rap dreams: becoming the Black Donald Glover.

I'm joking! I swear on my contempt for white supremacy and game nights. I know that Black people are not a monolith and I do indeed watch *Atlanta*. He's totes Black, but I do feel like white people didn't share him until his hair grew out more and he started looking like Billy Dee Williams exactly when his Lando Calrissian kicked in.

I admire Donald Glover's career because while we're not the same variety of Black man, we both share the quality of not being the ideal candidate for a successful mainstream male rapper. There are certain kinds of Black men you would typically associate with rap stardom, and they're not traditionally like Glover. I know Drake is also cited, but I think he ought to come with an asterisk because while Aubrey sings ear-pleasing tunes that are often de facto passive-aggressive odes to strippers who left him on read, he's a Canadian yet somehow manages to sound like he's from Houston or Memphis or London or South Africa or some part of the Caribbean at any given moment. He's a nice middle-class mixed child of God and a man who dresses like a villain from the blaxploitation hit *Coffy* actively trying to blend in. That's why Donald Glover might one day cuss me smooth out for that joke, but at least I didn't call him an incredibly talented hood hopper.

I liked Childish Gambino's "This Is America," but I don't want to have to explain racism to white people. I have to constantly make arguments for myself and marginalized people as a whole in my work now. Glover, who performs under the moniker, made it look fun, but I strongly doubt it would be any less worrisome for me with a drumbeat and cute choreography. Let the Negro wunderkind have it.

I just want to be a nigga.

A nigga without substance.

Who just smiles all day.

You know the way a post–prison release, post–fitness journey Gucci Mane just smiles?

I want to be able to smile like Gucci Mane.

And I want to dress like 2 Chainz.

Truth be told, "the gay 2 Chainz" is the vision I accompanied my rap dreams revelation with.

2 Chainz went to college, so he can read, but Tity Boi isn't necessarily attempting to tantalize your brain cells with his rhymes. It's bars about being rich, wearing Versace, and rapping better than everyone. I can think of no greater paradise.

It's not about trying to be like a straight man. I just can't think of any other rappers who I grew up with having more fun than southern ones.

I have long had a title for my first mixtape: *Cognac and Celexa*.

Cognac in honor of the type of brown liquor most beloved by Black elders, and Celexa, my favorite antidepressant. Obviously, I've been stewing over my track listing for several years. I already know I want to sample Rihanna rapping "I bet you niggas gon' be like, 'Bitch, that's my fucking song'" for a lead single. Speaking of niggas, I already know what subjects I want to cover: being a nigga; being that nigga; being a nigga from Houston; being that nigga from Houston; being a rich nigga; being a rich nigga that's that nigga. I'll be sure to include the additional required nods to pride, greed, lust, envy, gluttony, wrath, and sloth.

I do want to switch it up in some respects. I know every now and then a mainstream rapper wants to work with a gospel artist in order to make their Black moms and Jesus happy, but I'd like to try a spin on that. Instead of seeking conversion therapy or entertaining sociopathy in order to tell the lie that I am straight in order to impress Donnie McClurkin, I'll find some wayward Christian to croon about committing a little sin like sodomy instead. I imagine none of the premier Winans would agree to this, but there has to be a third cousin who can sing a lil' bit with enough hot tea around that would agree to joining me in sharing a heathen's tale. If not, we can find somebody to yell like a Baptist in the background for effect.

I would also love to make a couple of mumble rap records. For people like me who can't always remember the words anyway but still want to sing along with everyone at the day party you said you'd only stay an hour at before you lose your entire Sunday, I find this to be an olive branch to the wider community.

I have some things to consider.

Originally, I planned to make my rap name Youngsinick. It's a nod to my old blog, *The Cynical Ones*, and a post I made where I first gave hints of wanting to rap. That is to say, if you believe including in the post a picture of me fitted with foil in the front of my teeth as a preview of a grill constitutes only a hint. There were haters in the comments, too, but I think they wanted better for the name. I can't go by "young" anymore either. If Jeezy let go of it, I have to follow in his infinite wisdom.

I haven't settled on whether or not I wanted to play a character à la Rick Ross. Through him, an ex–corrections officer who took on the persona of a drug dealer named Rick Ross (who will contact you on Facebook if you are a member of the press to tell you the "real story," FYI), I learned you can be fake as fuck and claim being a real one all the same. Insert the Rick Ross grunt here, which, by the way, used to be my text message alert. That's no dig to Rick Ross, but a salute to a dedicated thespian. I'll more than likely opt to be only myself at the club after the orders of tequila and soda have kicked in. I want to be the kind of rapper who dances on tables at clubs anyway.

The only problem is there is no version of any of these men in mainstream hip-hop. Donald Glover is different, but he's straight so there's more space for him than there would be for me to be absorbed by mainstream rap culture rather than having to gnaw at it in order to break through. It's much harder for people to envision a gay male commercial rapper.

That's not to say gay rappers don't exist. Plenty of them do. Mykki Blanco. Lelf.

Lil Nas X. Cakes Da Killa. Big Freedia. Many others. None of them are the same, and each of them is breaking down barriers. Still, hip-hop and queer hip-hop remain relatively separate, through no fault of their own. That doesn't negate gay rappers' successes or suggest they won't break down even great barriers in their careers; it's just that being pioneering is as challenging as it is rewarding.

They ultimately have to contend with the homophobia that may no longer be strangling hip-hop, but much as in the greater society that hip-hop reflects, is still enough to make things only bearable, not equitable.

On one end, I can appreciate a rapper like Young Thug for wearing frocks and being comfortable enough to refer to fellow straight male rapper friends as "hubby," "my love," and "babe" without much concern. He's been met with slight ridicule from older rappers like Snoop Dogg on occasion, but for the most part, he's relatively free to be. That's good for him but frustrating given that if he were actually gay, the responses would be different.

That homophobia is informed by misogyny, and given that mainstream hip-hop culture has yet to fully reconcile with that, I have doubts about how good it can ever conceivably get.

Take XXXTentacion, the pregnant woman–beating rapper who also beat up a gay inmate and bragged about it, and how promptly he was canonized after he was killed. I'm aware an entire generation of younger people admires him, but if we're to truly speak about progress in hip-hop, what does it say that someone capable of that not only was born in 1998, but saw his misogyny, homophobia, and violent outbursts glossed over the same way the behavior of the other monsters before him was?

Now compare that with the living gay rapper ILoveMakonnen, who in 2015 came out via Twitter: "As a fashion icon, I can't tell u about everybody else's closet, I can only tell u about mine, and it's time I've come out. And since y'all love breaking news, here's some old news to break, I'm gay. And now I've told u about my life, maybe u can go life [sic] yours."

I knew ILoveMakonnen as that dude who mumbled "club goin' up on a Tuesday" on the 2014 single "Tuesday." In theory, that's the gist of my preference for sound, but overall ILoveMakonnen is more of indie rock, come down from the high music. Different strokes. Regardless, his coming out was supposed to initiate a shift.

In an interview with *Rolling Stone*, Migos responded to Makonnen's coming out. "They supported him?" questioned Quavo. His cohorts Offset and Takeoff were more direct in their responses. "This world is not right," said Takeoff, while Offset said that the support only came "because the world is fucked up."

These comments agitated me because I love Migos's music and didn't need them to become the audible answer to my favorite combo at Chick-fil-A. And when I say love, I would consider it an honor and a privilege to become the Jean Terrell of Migos after Quavo leaves for good because he thinks he's the Beyoncé of the trio when he is their Camila Cabello, which is fine but not the same no matter how one tries to spin it.

After being dragged up and down the internet over their comments, the group released a statement. "We always been about being original and staying true. Staying true to yourself goes a long way," the note read. "We are all fans of Makonnen's music and we wish he didn't feel like he ever had to hide himself. We feel the world is fucked up that people feel like they have to hide and we're asked to comment on someone's sexuality."

They would go on to trip over themselves again for various reasons, but I get the sense that while they may not especially hate ILoveMakonnen or wish him harm because of his sexuality, they would rather not be associated with him all the same, so as not to invite any speculation about themselves.

Some years later, ILoveMakonnen confirmed as much in an interview: "I haven't had any vocal support from any of them. You know what I mean? . . . Just like, we accept you and we fuck with you still . . . Don't think that it's all good in the hood, because it's still not until people can man up and face themselves. Then they could face me."

I feel bad for him. I feel bad for whoever comes after him. And the one after that. It's going to take people a long time to see a gay man as the kind of rapper he wants to be seen as: a rapper that happens to be gay, not the gay rapper. It's right on par with the goal of getting some men to see gay men as men. *Any day now.*

In 2013, Talib Kweli did an interview with *Mother Jones* and was asked about the difficulties in a gay mainstream rapper fully breaking through. "There just needs to be a gay rapper— he doesn't have to be flamboyant, just a rapper who identifies as gay—who's better than everybody," he explained.

I don't want to be the Sojourner Truth of gay rappers; I would have a much better time being the Slim Thug and Saweetie of them.

"I feel if I lacked morals and had a harder face then rapping would be a lyrically promising career for me," my ridiculous friend Corey told me. "We are all one face tattoo away from experiencing our own rap dreams."

I liked the idea of becoming a rapper because I can't think of anything better than being paid handsomely to act like those niggas. I forgot I can't be a nigga in hip-hop because I'm a faggot. That reminds me of all of the other rooms that I've been in where I'm paid faint praise before being told that despite all the positives going for me, I'm just not the right fit for the position I know they associate more with straight men. It's been relayed to me in reference to opportunities for my other, nonmusical dreams. Some make more effort than others to disguise their real grievances. My voice. My mannerisms. What they convey. It's a recurring theme of checking too many boxes, but when the identities are separated, you are considered too much of one and not enough of the other.

When I think of being a rapper that way, it all becomes a lot less fun. I already know what limitations are placed on me by virtue of existing. I don't need it pouring into my fantasy life. It's too bad, though. I am certain I would make a pretty solid rapper of so-so skill level that makes up for it thanks to ear, songwriting ability, and if all else fails, sympathy and payola.

Too bad I'm too aware of all of the reasons it couldn't work.

This is what La must have meant about me being too smart to be a rapper, though I still swear that I'm ignorant enough to make it work if I ever got the chance.

FLOAT ON

His smile seemed to convey amusement but belied what was really behind it. His giddiness appeared to be sparked by the sight of me—me, reflecting an image he was routinely accused of presenting. The one he loathed with great vigor but was guilty of exhibiting each and every single time he was called on it. In the moments after he watched me hop out of Kim's car and walk back into the house, he caught the glaze in my eyes, and responded with a smile that frustrated me. He knew. He could tell. I never wanted to give him that satisfaction.

I was back in Houston for the second time when it happened.

I had vacated my old apartment in LA because my second roommate had left and I did not want another. She had been a nice person, but passive-aggressive, and with a cat. I could deal with a passive-aggressive person, but when she mentioned bringing her pet, I'd been hesitant—until she swore she would keep him in her room or in that massive contraption she bought for him. She was lying, and that whiny little monster was a headache to constantly clean up after. He was probably cleaner than she was, though. The two of them would forever ruin roommates for me.

I was looking for another place (all my own), only to run into a few hiccups: being let go of one position where I had made most of my monthly intake and running into trouble getting paid for the work that was supposed to supplant it. It was more "human error" that humans of decency would have fixed sooner, but alas. All I could do was hope my money would come when promised, and if not, may the folks responsible fall into a lake of fire. Very Old Testament form of vengeance to be sure, but to quote my favorite corrections officer turned rapper and undeclared thespian, Rick Ross, "God forgives. I don't."

The delay in pay led to me crashing on a friend's couch for what was supposed to be a week but turned into five or six. I was forever grateful for the generosity, but it didn't take long for me to realize that I was wearing my friend thin. I wasn't junky or loud or intruding; I was just there longer than advertised. Sorry.

By the time everything got sorted out, the apartment I'd planned to move to was still available, but during the wait I'd questioned the purpose of staying there given how unhappy I had grown living in that city. One friend in particular, Mitzi, flat-out told me on a phone call, "Why are you still acting like you don't want to live in New York? Move already." The only one stopping me was myself.

I got out of my own way. The decision to stay in Houston longer than originally planned had been one heavily weighed. My immediate plan was to drive back to Houston, and for about a month just be still, before heading to New York City, where I knew I belonged at this point in my life and career, to find an apartment. But given the months that preceded me leaving LA, I eventually decided to take up the suggestion that I pause myself if only for a little while.

Moving back after college had been one thing; that was relatively normal, especially after what two terms of President George W. Bush did to the economy. But a repeat offense? That could potentially signal that I'd failed. Even though I returned with more money and more work, to be at home at twenty-eight, even if temporarily? I already felt like a fuckup being in this bind at this age. Did I want to feel like an even bigger fuckup?

Worse, home was a chaotic place where not much had changed and most of it showed no willingness to change. Why subject myself to that at length? Because I needed to save as much money as possible before some other jackass in accounts payable screwed me over, some other media company imploded on a whim, or some other unforeseen event happened and catapulted me back into another dire situation.

I wasn't especially social the second time around. I was focused. I was adamant about making clear this was not a permanent shift, but a strategic move for the greater good. I tried to behave as such in terms of how I lived, worked, and spent money. I went to the Vinson Neighborhood Library to write. Not the old location across the street from the post office. The new one—the one built a few minutes up from that. It's so nice. It reminds you of the new building you'd see pop up in the hood at the conclusion of some white savior movie tied to educating inner city youth.

The library kept weird hours—something about city budgets—but she was a cute, quiet location to focus. There were quiet moments at my parents' house, but only if my mom was the only other person there. Everyone else was more lively, which you enjoyed, but not when focus was required. So if I wasn't at Vinson Library trying to focus, you could find me at the Starbucks on Main Street. It had a lot of car traffic, given its proximity to the loop and Texas Medical Center, but not a lot of people ever planted themselves there for long. I wasn't in New York, Los Angeles, or D.C. anymore. There were other places with centralized air-conditioning to spend your time on the side of town I was used to.

I would go out sometimes. Mainly happy hours, though. Not out of cheapness—the liquor is cheaper in the South no matter where it is served or what time it is served—but because of the emphasis on avoiding staying out too late because I wanted to tackle as much work as possible to make as much money as I could to get the hell out the city and back to my plans.

It wasn't a bad choice. I saved money and paid off debts from the time. To that end, thank you, Mom and Dad, for not charging me rent. Some parents do that. I'm glad my parents did not do that. They would never do that. I'm forever grateful of that, weirdness of the situation be damned.

To stay there rent-free didn't mean there wasn't a price to pay, however. I had to live with him again, in his house. He and my mom might not have taken money from me, but being there left me prone to him finding ways to take up space in my head—whether or not that was inadvert or intentional was moot.

We almost fought after I called him a bitch over the way he spoke to my mom. Gone were the days of waiting for him to strike; with my age, added weight and height, along with residual anger, confrontation felt like the key to retribution and subsequent bliss. But that was not the best move for either of us. He needed to chill and I needed to scale back my resentment.

Over time, I learned to have compassion for my father. To not judge his alcoholism solely through the lens of the pain it brought to his wife and children, but to recognize that he himself was hurting. I learned to accept that while nothing he revealed ever excused his actions, he did suffer from a disease that can be directly traced back to trauma. Being able to recognize that his fallibility, no matter how high I believed it ranked, was directly attributed to circumstance rather than being innately horrible, I was able to meet him where he was without most of the resentment. I say most because realistically, all isn't forgiven; merely put into context.

As always, he offered gestures by way of food. He made me turkey wings. Turkey wings can infinitely make a bad situation better if smoked and baked correctly. He likes when he does something that elicits happiness from us. So he made turkey wings often.

By now I had already started to be receptive to him asking me to drink some of his liquor, if I wanted to. He wanted me to drink it. It was his way of bonding. I was never going to be like the men outside who were easier for him to relate to than me, but I could at least accept this gesture. He kept the liquor in water bottles in the cabinet. Easier to transport, I guess.

They were in the cabinet that was right above the microwave. My mom kept a lot of medicine over the microwave. My dad called his alcohol his "medicine" from time to time. His medicine was Paul Masson, Jack Daniel's, and maybe Crown Royal. Only in California have I seen the medicine of my mom and the medicine of my dad sold at the same location.

I sort of liked that he liked that I accepted his offer and also invited him to try whatever liquor I got from the liquor store across the street. I have a thing for trying out whatever alcohol a rapper is affiliated with. He would try whatever because he is a drinker.

It was fine, or as fine it could conceivably be anyway. What wasn't so fine was him spotting me impacted by the effects of marked down well liquor. That threatened the peace accord between us that I had drafted in my head. It's one thing to have a drink with you, it's another for you to look at me and think I'm drunk—like you.

I understand many men start as boys who idolize their fathers and want to be like them. I've added nuance to my father both in my work and my real-life conclusions that have informed it, but that doesn't mean I ever wanted to do anything that suggested I was a reflection of him. And if I ever did, I didn't want him to see it up close and in person. So much for that. Why was I drinking $1 tequila in Pearland anyway?

When he saw me and clocked me, he couldn't wait to tell someone—specifically the one who often led the charge on making the obvious even more pronounced.

He told my mom that he saw me looking tipsy. Well, that nigga doesn't use words like "tipsy." He likely used the descriptor "drunk" or some variation that only someone within his demo—uh, aging thuggish Negro but with heavy country overtones given regional background—would say to my mom. I wondered if he was aiming for a gotcha moment.

She described the scene as such anyway, which is why when she told me the next day what he had said, she did so dismissively.

"He just wanted to finally say he wasn't the only one around here drinking too much."

I felt the same, hence my irritation. In my mind, I could

never, ever be like him. Even if he didn't mean it that way, and to give credit to him, perhaps he just thought I looked funny as hell sloshed or whatever—our history didn't call for humor, so no matter the motive, it was going to be troubling to me.

As the child of an alcoholic with good knowledge of how drug abuse and alcohol addiction snatched the soul of many a male Arceneaux, it took me longer to start drinking compared to many of my friends. Outside of a sip of church wine, a wine cooler at a high school graduation party, and a sip of some consenting uncle's adult beverage once or twice at a holiday function, I didn't have a sip of the stuff until I was twenty-one. It wasn't self-awareness about the virtues of self-restraint; my mama didn't let me go anywhere in high school and I took a while to adjust to college socially.

When I did start drinking, it was like a fish—true to form for men of my familial lineage. I noticed that unless I hadn't eaten that day, it would take quite a bit of alcohol consumption for me to feel any effect. I had to learn how to gauge my alcohol intake, but for the most part, it didn't have the negative consequences for me that it did for others around me.

Booze loosened me up a bit. It toned down my demeanor, which did not generally present as outwardly jovial. That's my way of saying it tempered that resting bitch face I'm accused of having. I talked to boys who wanted to talk to me but were not going to make the first move. It got me to dance.

I did not like to drink my feelings. I tried that once—the first time I moved back home and was sad and mopey over the state of my life. I was also mad about some man I should have let go of 'cause it wasn't like he was ever going to admit he had feelings for me, too. It was early in the afternoon—probably a little after twelve—when I went to the liquor store to get what was ultimately a liter of Belvedere. I went home, turned down the lights in the living room, and went to the main computer in the house and turned on Amy Winehouse's *Frank* album.

That album is fantastic, but the following vision was less than stellar: me, suddenly on the ground crying like an idiot while holding the bottle. If I could go back in time, I would stand over myself, kick me ever so slightly, and lovingly say, "Get your goofy ass the fuck up."

It was so overly dramatic, but I react remarkably poorly to lingering feelings of being trapped.

There is a fine line between having a naturally high tolerance and possessing a lack of impulse control. When you turn to alcohol for comfort, you can be convicted swiftly on the latter. And while I could understand how my dad became someone who moved in such fashion, I had the attitude that I was above that.

I have had many drunken moments, but I learned. Drink water in between drinks. Take BC Powder before and/or after you're done drinking to prevent hangovers. I have tried to tell so many people about the benefits of BC Powder. I cannot believe they haven't given me an endorsement deal yet. Someday, I'll be the one their ad execs are wishing for.

That was all about coming up with ways to deal with the physical effects of too much drinking, but I also considered how to mentally not let booze get ahold of me. I didn't consider that that wasn't making me better than anyone, only more equipped to handle a looming problem. Because I could intellectualize the situation. It counted for something, but not nearly as much as I used to believe it did.

Life did get me together, gradually. I'd soon learn that I wasn't immune from the circumstances that cause people— my father—to pick up a bottle full of a substance that altered their state of mind. It simply took more living and, ultimately, trial and error to realize not only that any feelings of difference between me and those people were invalid, but that I was the bigger sucker for believing otherwise.

I have never genuinely wanted to try cocaine, but I used to get offended that no one ever offered me the opportunity to ruin my life. I doubt it was that D.A.R.E. essay competition I won way back in the 1990s. I just wanted to stunt at the assembly and eat pizza.

I think I give off judgmental vibes—probably because I can be judgmental—but I'm not a narc. I've had plenty of friends pop their lil' pills around me, and I didn't immediately begin quoting lyrics from "My Mind's Playing Tricks on Me" or singing the theme from *Cops*. At most, I'd say, "Pop that shit now 'cause just my luck we'll get pulled over and they'll blame me, not you, lady." I'll be damned if I die by a trigger-happy cop on the way to a gay club that I was told has termites.

I didn't judge the folks who dated drug dealers, either. I didn't grow up in Mayberry; mad people sell drugs. So long as you don't make me go on runs with you, be best.

It couldn't have been anyone recognizing that I was the child of an addict. People aren't that considerate, grow up. Whatever the case, no one ever directly asked me about cocaine until I was in my mid-twenties. The person who asked was an LA native; figures.

She picked me up for a day party and randomly asked me if I had ever done it. She asked in a leading way that suggested she was down if I was. And then she confirmed.

Girl. No. Hell no. But whatever rocks your boat and works

the middle is fine for you, but you know I don't need anything
that would make me even skinnier.

FINALLY.

She knew damn well I wasn't about to do that rich people's drug with her, but it's the thought that counts.

The only drug I had ever tried when she asked was weed.

That, too, took longer for me to try than it did most of the people I knew.

I had to have been about twenty-one at the time.

I made it a whole celebration with my best friend Kim.

We would go to Pappasito's to get takeout, and then we would go back to her house, where her mom would roll our blunts. At the time, her mom was not smoking, because of her job, but as evidenced by her rolling capabilities, she seemed to have had a special skill set in a past life. I had a good time, but it didn't become a habit as a result. At most, I would hit it if it were around at a house party. Outside of that, I avoided weed.

It wasn't until my early thirties that I tried something else.

It wasn't crystal meth. I'm too vain to allow my mug to give "My mug died five years ago, but my body won't give up the fight." It certainly wasn't heroin, or "her-ron" as Blacks of a certain age or speech pattern would say, because my uncle Daniel had a tragic end to his life messing around with that. Apologies to my fellow Houstonians, it wasn't lean, either. From what I gathered from my surroundings, lean made you very immobile, to the point where you just kind of sat there and packed on pounds. I was already big in the past and have suffered from strep throat so much that cough syrup could never provide any entertainment value, no matter the new-fangled concoction.

There are better ways for me to honor Houston: trashing

Dallas every chance I get, an unyielding commitment to the phrase "Mane, hol' up," and reminding everyone that Shipley's Do-Nuts is superior to all other donut chains.

What I did later try was Adderall, and it wasn't even for any fun-related reason. My use of it for the first time was borne out of slight desperation. I was not able to take off from writing full-time to write a full-fledged book, so on the advice of someone with a prescription, I told myself to give it a try to improve my concentration. It wasn't the first offering; that was also in Los Angeles, when a TV writer gave me a pill with a big grin on her face. I called her a crackhead in my mind and threw that shit away. (My bad, girl.)

This time, I didn't pass on it. My level of focus was not where it needed to be, and the mental exhaustion that comes with writing to the speed of the internet while trying to revisit and process one's own trauma felt overwhelming to a frequently overwhelmed person. So I used something that I knew wasn't an ideal substitute, but was the one readily available.

I learned later that I had basically taken the legal form of coke. I had taken pride in never trying a drug that had Rick James smacking folks up and always sweating his jheri curl out. Unfortunately, I now had to face a new truth: that I cannot take Adderall and feel above a coke whore. It would be like a Real Housewife looking down on a cast member of *Love & Hip Hop* because when you look at both at their core, they're all inebriated persons messing up some small business owner's restaurant wineglasses. Classism isn't cool, and neither is a drug hierarchy. #TheMoreYouKnow.

That aside, I do not like how I feel on Adderall. It serves its purpose, but I'm not the kind of person who needs so much help being wound up. It doesn't distract me from my problems either. If anything, it adds a hyper-awareness to them. I didn't have to worry about ever becoming addicted to regulated blow, because it didn't produce any joy or sense of distraction.

But I did have instant and growing fondness for when I used to come down from Adderall.

The same person who gave me some of his pills also gave me weed pills that I used to return my body and mind to a place in which I could rest. It's hard to describe it since it wasn't prescribed and thus explained to me carefully. I know the pills have cannabis in them, and doctors prescribed them to patients who needed to bolster their appetites and reestablish their sleeping patterns. I took them, much like the Adderall, as some kind of suburban-ass high.

Adderall did not become a regular thing for me, but weed slowly but surely did. It started with the pills and then led me to buying edibles. I got edibles because I wasn't ready to ask people to buy flowers. I also couldn't roll weed, an embarrassment to family members and other loved ones who have sold weed and consumed heavily around me, so there was that. But then I discovered oil cartridges and vape pens, along with cones, which made it far easier for the clueless to put something together and smoke without pathetic failure.

Fuck Jeff Sessions for a lifetime of reasons, but in this instance, for his aggressively anti-marijuana stance during his tenure as attorney general. He can suck on a Black dick while smoking OG Kush for all I care. Weed is not like other drugs; it's much more on par with alcohol and tobacco. However, the Keebler elf–looking neoconfederate's antagonism notwithstanding, I will concede that weed is a vice, and like many vices, it can be abused.

About a year into me getting high regularly, I recorded myself high. I wanted to hear how I sounded. I was hoping I sounded like I was floating on air the way Jhené Aiko does on her song "Sativa," a duet with the songbird of the rap duo Rae Sremmurd, Swae Lee. Aiko may have blocked me on Twitter for some unfortunate reason that ideally ends with a feature for me on her next single, but that doesn't stop me from pretending I can have a spiritual connection.

When I listened to what I recorded the next morning with a sober mind, I did not sound whispery and angelical; my voice suggested I was heading to the closest Chipotle on Europa with the assumption that given it was the smallest of the four Galilean moons orbiting Jupiter, it was sure to have the shortest line and I desperately need chorizo, as fast as humanly possible—and it was available for a limited time only!

Or to put it more plainly, I sounded like a smooth fool. But even with the lack of coherence or cognizance of what planet I was on at the time, I sounded a lot happier than I had been lately. Happier than I usually sound period, honestly.

I wrestle with admitting these words out loud and in print, but if total transparency were being demanded of me, I can admit it: I like being high.

I revel in it, if I'm being franker. It feels so good to sometimes be physically present but mentally somewhere that feels lighter. To not have your mind be so wrapped in all your fears and doubts and worries. To both physically and mentally feel as if a weight has been lifted for knowingly not forever, but at least for the time being. To have something in your life that can provide you an escape, temporary or not.

There are songs that I love to listen to while high. Mary J. Blige's "I Never Wanna Live Without You" sounds sublime in a standard state of my mind solely off the strength of how well her voice blends with Faith Evans's, but it's something even sweeter after it all starts to kick in. I think I can actually sing then—and I'm fine with needing to be high to think I can sing. I feel equally as good listening to works from some of my other favorite hip-hop soul divas, like Future and Travis Scott, when in the thick of this pursued haze.

For someone that has not ever felt completely in control of their life, as foolish as it sounds, when I get high, I feel freer than I've ever felt. My past doesn't feel like it's in the way. My present struggles—the debt tied around my neck more than anything—aren't centered like they so often are.

No matter how self-driven I am or how determined I find myself to be to reach my dreams and create better for myself and those I love, ambition and resilience are not enough sustenance. Your problems—real and imagined—catch up to you. The trauma you carry and continue to leave unsettled will weigh you down. There's only so much your mind and body can take. We're not always as in control of our minds and bodies anyway, right? Depression told me so anyway.

I know this all too well. I get so tired. So very tired. I worry it may never end, no matter what I do. Sometimes, you worry so much and your fears and trauma trample so hard over you that you just don't want to get up. You don't know what to do anymore. Everything else you used to do no longer works. You don't have the desire to try anything else. Then people pile their problems on you because you serve as so many people's security blanket. You present as the strong one. The one that perseveres again and again. Because that's who you are to people. Not enough of them care enough about you to ask how you are holding up—they need you to serve their needs.

It's too much. So you get high. You get high because you just want to float on, float on, float on. It feels so good to just float sometimes. It's so much better than anything else I've just described. That's why you keep getting high. You want to remember what you feel like when you aren't weighed down by the heft of your challenges.

And you have so many options for getting high now. So many that you don't have to be lazy and lethargic while high. You can use sativa products. Hell, they even have products that promise to help you stay focused and creative even as you are under the influence. It's perfect. In moderation anyway.

I know the reason why I started getting high might prompt a "duh" from some, given I got one in real time from a friend. But it can be difficult for a child of an addict to admit they like being under the influence. We know escapism sounds nice until it inches toward what comes to be viewed as dependence.

It didn't help that I hadn't used any antidepressants in years. Celexa is my bitch, but my health coverage has thrown a wrench in me not only finding a decent doctor, but making the medication affordable—as it previously was for a much lower monthly premium. The weed man has been easier to get to than a pharmacist at CVS, and cheaper, even if I know he's overcharged me a little bit for those cartridges. And I don't know if I ever want to be back on medication—at least without therapy anyway.

Weed was more accessible, so by default, inherently more functional.

I was getting high every now and then, and then it became an everyday thing. I learned to be high and functional. It took longer than I would care to admit to see that sounded eerily similar to my father. My dad made a habit of separating himself from other alcoholics by constantly arguing about his functionality. He maintained a specific image of what an addict looks like. For him, that was the buffoonish drunk. Someone who couldn't hold down a job, maintain a relationship, be loved. No, he was a "professional." That was a way of acknowledging one's excessive drinking without confessing to being like all the others who consume too much alcohol. You're not them; you can hold your liquor.

I knew as a kid that he convinced himself of this in order to rationalize his drinking and maintain his status quo. What I couldn't foresee was that that habit—a generational trait at this point—could be duplicated easily by me. The one who swore he would never become an alcoholic stood firm by that promise, though only with an asterisk attached to those bragging rights. No, I'm nobody's drunk, but I was self-medicating the way he and so many others I knew were. I'm not walking around here like a zombie looking for a hit, but I wonder if my weed man started to look at me the same way a bartender looks at someone coming around too frequently.

Look at me, sounding like ever the professional.

Lil' Wayne is responsible for my favorite addiction-themed songs: "Me and My Drank" and "I Feel Like Dying." On the former, I am drawn to the way he frames the dependency— it's kind of a generational equivalent to "Mary Jane," a nod to Houston rapper Big Moe and his iconic "Barre Baby." It's fun and only makes me think about the fun parts of being high out of my mind. "I Feel Like Dying" doesn't make me any less aware of the pleasure I associate to smoking, but it's the repetition of the feeling after it's down that's a bit haunting even if I sway through it.

"Wish I could give you this feeling. I feel like buying. And if my dealer don't have no more then I feel like dying."

I don't want to ever feel that way. I always have to remember to never allow myself to get to the point in which I feel that way. But that sounds like something that can become easily forgettable. I have to keep that in mind at all times, too.

Or maybe stop altogether?

This is not the part where I say I had an epiphany and learned to drink the non-psychedelic CBD tea now sold at the formerly hood grocer turned market for onslaught of new white neighbors. This is not a script to a forthcoming after-school special.

I still hit up the weed man because I like supporting entrepreneurship. And I still like getting high.

But I do have a newfound understanding of how people— notably those in my life whose addictions impacted me negatively—can fall. It's one thing to intellectualize it, but critical thinking and analysis don't make you *feel it*. To feel it is to make you empathetic in ways you previously thought were implausible. It's another way to understand the condition. I get it now. Oh, how I get it in ways I never understood years ago.

My dad and I are not two men who have conversations at length. We call each other to check in, but we spend a lot of the short time talking about the weather. But though he may not know how to talk to me about my problems, he's displayed a knack for being able to clock when I have one. He's always been able to hear me say "I'm all right" and know when I don't mean it.

I said "I'm all right" a lot of the time I was back home for the second time. I didn't mean it most of the time. I was hurting. For a lot of varied reasons, but hurt is hurt. As my father, it makes sense that he could see the same in his son. As someone else hurting, it makes even more sense that he could spot something off in me.

I wish he knew how to better communicate. I don't fault him for not knowing how to. His parents didn't teach him. But I wish he did. I always wanted to know when was the first time he drank and when was the first time he needed to drink. And if the shift was swift or did it take a while?

I wish I knew how to better communicate. I could ask him so many questions, but I have never made the attempt. I've always assumed any personal question asked would have the conversation directly go south, becoming triggering for both of us, and as a result, hostile—maybe too hostile. Such fear is rational to have based on my experience, but I never bothered to put such a theory to the test. That's a shame because the ghosts of all his sins are what's been chasing me. Maybe it's too late for him, but I wonder if he knows the best way to shake those demons now?

I might have read far too much into his laughter at me rolling into the house drunk. I won't dismiss charges of it being slightly shady in its appearance, but it might have extended beyond that. Maybe, just maybe, he saw someone he knew was hurting, too, and for a little bit, it looked as if some of what ailed him had momentarily disappeared based on a practice that for him was routine.

I'll never know. We'll never talk about it. It's not our way. But I needed to be knocked off my high horse a bit. It's better that I finally accept that, for all my protests, I am my father's son. Intellect and access do not negate genetics or how cycles are created and cemented. I can end up exactly like him. I've already proven so.

I am him. I am his child. I acknowledge that in title, but intentionally distance that reality whenever assessing my traits. But I am who I am in part because of him. Acquiescing to that truth is long overdue.

I have not completely weaned myself off of weed. I'm not sure I ever will. I don't believe I have to until it gets too bad. I have not settled on what "too bad" means yet, but I do keep that smirk in a mental back pocket as a reminder to not allow myself to keep floating for too long.

I have to conquer all that leads me to rush for an escape.

In the meanwhile, I've at least cut back a bit on consumption. I need to actively remember that it has been helpful in a time of need but I don't need it. The connect started to overcharge anyway. I understand supply and demand, but you low key were already overcharging so I demand some chill—you from your prices or me from paying them frequently. Guess I should be happy he never had a big sale that left me compelled to stock up.

And thank goodness I never learned how to roll. I have long carried the shame of that with me, but that was God and Beyoncé sparing me black lips. I give them the glory for that.

They're the ones truly there for me when I need them the most.

I LOVE INSTAGRAM. IT SOMETIMES MAKES ME WANT TO DIE.

have developed a bit of a routine over the years. I've always been an early riser, but as I've gotten older (I've officially tipped into my mid-thirties, which is not technically old, but in gay years the age strongly suggests that I'm two Cardi B album releases away from needing a cane and a living will), I've started to wake up earlier than ever. So just about every single day of the week, whether I like it or not, I wake up around 6 a.m.

If it's a weekday, I immediately turn on *Morning Joe*. During the second half of the Obama administration's sequel, I told myself no one's masochism should begin this early in the day, so I decided to end my suffering already and stop watching. Note that even though they were no longer part of my morning routine, I continued to hope that Joe and Mika would go ahead and get married already.

Then Sweet Potato Saddam was technically elected President of the United States. After tripping through the five stages of acceptance (I mean, white people gon' white people), anger (okay, I'm still angry), bargaining (uh, I watched other people give Jill Stein money for that "recount," if that counts), depression (I'm actually still depressed), and acceptance (he remains only white folks' president as far as I'm concerned), I started watching *Morning Joe* again. Confirming old habits do indeed die hard, it continues to only take me about five minutes to become enraged by something said on that show. The likely culprits remain Joe Scarborough and Mike Barnicle, but you can add Donny Deutsch to the list.

I'll stick it out to the eight o'clock hour, when they replay whatever it was that had me hit mute to begin with. Once I officially give myself some space from the daybreak punditry, I mute the TV again, grab my phone, and turn to Instagram as I start freshening up and getting ready for my day. People tend to assume I like Twitter the most because it's the one I post the most frequently on. In actuality, if I weren't a writer for the internet, I'd probably use Twitter the least. I'm a news junkie, so sure, the ability to glean the news cycle on Twitter is cool, but I could do without the pointless relationship-focused debates that are never-ending; and the rampant bigotry of far too many ghouls left free to roam and troll (both real and imagined by a Russian) because the tech bros fear the alt-right or lean their way and won't explicitly admit such; and especially the people who may fancy themselves as activists but are nothing more than alarmists exploiting the works of others and the tragedies that push them to take action.

I'm tired from even conjuring up the bad spirits.

As part of the original group of Black Twitter users who made the service a thing and piqued the interests of white people in media who had never had a real insight into the id of a certain segment of the Black population, I, too, lament the "good old days" of Twitter when it seemed more fun. Twitter feels like work for me now. I know because the minute I start tweeting enough about a given topic, I'll be asked if I would like to expand those 140 to 280 characters into an 800-word piece. The game is the game and I have bills to pay, but when you know how much of what you say will be taken largely in professional terms, it's less fun. Twitter maintains some levels of entertainment value, but there is a toxicity throughout the platform that makes it increasingly easier to look away.

But I don't think of Instagram as work. I will post about my work on it, but I don't consider my usage there to be work-focused. It's the only social media platform where I am not expected to be so *on* as a writer. Well, there was Snapchat, but after Instagram did a copy and paste with the main reason to use Snapchat, the masses ghosted them. I'd say millions of us owe Snapchat an apology, but that would only make Vine jealous. To Snapchat's credit, they remain the better app to use if you want to digitally paint your face or look like a labradoodle, for those keeping score. And ho shit . . . allegedly.

Anyhow, I can post an Instastory of me acting a fool on the weekend with my friends or cousin and it will be received in the unserious way it was intended to be. The same goes for my impromptu reviews of the original *Dynasty* after a snowstorm led to canceled weekend plans, which were followed by procrastination that went on to produce a marathon viewing featuring Diahann Carroll and Joan Collins. I would try to recapture the original magic here, but like Lauryn Hill, I'm too weary of following up sheer brilliance so you'll have to excuse me. I will at least state that I have never in my life been so amused by overly dramatic acting (shout out to Linda Evans and her portrayal of Krystle Carrington) and the beneficiaries of Reaganomics.

I like that Instagram is less text-heavy. There is plenty of text to be found across Instagram to be sure, but if I see someone post one of those faux inspirational word memes that sound like Dr. Seuss with dementia, I quietly judge that person, select mute this user, and scroll right on by. I go for the pictures. Not to soil my reputation as an upstanding member of the literary committee ("ratchet eloquence" as someone once said in an Instagram DM), but sometimes it's just nice to look at pictures and video. Pictures and video of elephants, ass, and food are all comforting.

There are other benefits to consider.

Instagram can teach me how to make dishes that aren't as complicated as I initially thought—though I will make it a point to add seasoning to my food because I wasn't raised to deny myself flavor. But I like learning about other cultures. How else would I have known how much white people like big blocks of white bread and cheese (the yellower, the better) for their quick meals?

Either there were far more fitness trainers than I ever realized prior to Instagram or Instagram led to a surge of personal trainers and fitness people in pursuit of a social media–driven hustle, but whatever the case, there are a lot of videos that help me figure out how to go into the gym and leave as if I kind of had an idea of what I was doing.

And there's lots of entertainment value. Yo, niggas love sharing a meme! Not to sound like a Gulf Coast elitist, but I don't find most of these memes at all comical. They're unimaginative and my LOL palate is, respectfully, higher. (I recognize that people who know me reading this will continue to send me those dumb-ass memes anyway. I love you more.)

I hate most of the memes I've been sent because not only are they not funny to me, but they typically need an editor. I suffer enough already skimming inane op-eds written by twenty-somethings or white male hacks in their fifties who would have benefitted from working with an editor that cared. But, since I don't like to be a spoiler, I try to always play along and feign laughter. Call me a fake-ass bitch for doing so if you must, but they feel seen and heard and I feel like Meryl Streep in any performance—never mind it's realistically more along the lines of Tommy "Tiny" Lister, Jr., as "T-Lay" in Master P's *I Got the Hook Up*; point is, I put on to make others happy. I'm so generous.

Instagram is a much better dating app than anything else I've tried. Grindr left me with scars and bedbugs. Jack'd had someone trying to get me caught out there and ready to jump into the streets like old Kelis. Tinder is like me trying to get at a hologram passing the time.

Can someone explain to me what is the point of matching someone and never planning to speak to them? If by chance you do speak to them, chances are slim that you ever engage them in person. For all of the people I've matched on Tinder, I have only gone on a single Tinder date.

He was some Black boy who lived in Williamsburg and taught yoga, but ultimately wanted to work in film or something arts-adjacent. He went to the same liberal arts college as a friend, who, after I noticed the connection, told me that she intended to try and set us up. We met at a spiffy pizza place on the Lower East Side that is now closed (R.I.P. to a real one). He told me he liked pizza, only he needed somewhere that had vegan options. Someone else put me onto this spot, but that wasn't this dude's business.

I found him even more attractive in person. It helped that he was smart and good at conversing. I thought the date was going well until he abruptly mentioned having just gone through a breakup and not being in the space to be actively dating someone right now.

If you're this person, do humanity a favor and stay your ass at home. Try crying and masturbating in the dark. Don't let your pain beget someone else's waste of time. It wasn't a total loss: the lamb sausage pizza was to die for and shit.

That date was several years ago, but guess who I stumbled across again on Instagram? He looked fit and flexible as ever, so I was tempted to slide into his DMs. But the more I scrolled down, the more the page reminded me that as good as he looked, he was more or less a beautiful gluten-free granola bar that would irritate me eventually.

Another point goes to Instagram for being a fine way to sniff out incompatibility.

I used to write against people looking up the social media of someone they recently met before getting to know them in person, but never mind. Seek out all the warning signs one way or another all you want. In nosily scrolling through his post, I found someone else that turned out to be worth spending some time with. Who doesn't love a platform that provides strong referrals?

I continue to scroll through Tinder while on the toilet, so my ability to match with people without ever yielding another actual date remains intact, but I've learned from others that it's not totally my fault, as it's happened often to them, too. For whatever reason—New York, me, men are awful—Instagram works much more efficiently than Tinder for that type of pursuit.

When it's not helping me connect to new and interesting people that conjure impure thoughts, it is also adept at helping me maintain minimal contact with people I have no plan of seeing in real life ever again. Yes, girl, I loved you in AP History, but I do not want to reminisce over happy hour margaritas at Taco Cabana whenever I am back in Houston, about something that happened around the time "Bootylicious" originally dropped. Just take the likes and let it be. That sounds so mean, but I still don't want to go.

I do appreciate the mess value of Instagram, too. By mess, I mean the Shade Room and the people arguing in the Shade Room for reasons I cannot explain and have opted not to try, for the sake of preserving my amusement. And I'll forever be intrigued that Instagram is also one big-ass virtual flea market and time-sensitive infomercial. I have never seriously considered wearing a corset, but dammit, if Mrs. Gucci Mane can look like that by hiring a waist trainer, maybe I need one? I'll try that over the diuretic tea all of the reality stars and fledging R&B singers pretend is the key to their weight loss. I do respect everyone's #fitnessjourney, however.

I'm on Instagram every morning. And afternoon. And evening. It's become a daily habit. I'm checking it not necessarily every nanosecond, but it's too much all the same. I know this thanks to my iPhone that sends me a weekly reminder of how much I squander my time staring at a screen, and which apps sucked up the largest percentage of those hours.

Yet I wouldn't say I am addicted to Instagram, though I can acknowledge that it can be addicting. I'd say my activity is rooted in trying to find ways to not be stuck in total solitary mode. I work from home, which means I don't get to socialize with people outside of social media during a lot of the workweek. I work a lot. Working from home can be fun, but it is not as fun as it sounds.

I need escapes like everyone else. I do go to the gym, but I don't want to talk to people there. I want to lift and bop to ho tunes in peace. That's supposed to be my escape from humanity's nuisances.

Social media is intended to provide connections. I'm not a fan of being disconnected, so I value outlets to make connections with people—especially in my adult life, where it has become harder to make connections of any sort with new people. I love Instagram for giving me quick bites of, if not real intimacy, something in proximity to it until I can go do hood rat things with my friends in real life.

If I were an addict, I'd be an addict in great company. There are people who will respond to an IG DM faster than a text, FaceTime, or if in a throwback mood, a phone call, after it is brought to their attention, once you've make a second effort, that you did indeed call on purpose. I can get off Instagram long enough to entertain texts or take phone calls from a limited list of people. With respect to FaceTime, though, I prefer to be given a proper warning. I loathe unsolicited FaceTimes—my friends could care less, so I end up making time for those, too.

And when I'm with friends—especially on the weekend—I don't use the app as much. I'm old-fashioned in that I prefer spending time with people. I also like to call people by the names their parents gave them. I scroll too much on Instagram, but I don't monitor my follow count, I don't call people by their IG names in public, and I try not to theme conversations around Instagram heavily. Should I ever end up one of those Instagays that post their bodies all the time only to get blocked after some bitchy gay reports them for violating the terms of service, I would absolutely not launch a new account with a bio listing my original follower count. Yeah, there are people who engage in such antics. God bless them.

Speaking of follower counts, I have never felt the urge to buy followers either. I understand why some might believe they need to do that—if they are chasing #influencer money or have some other careerist intention. It looks stupid to have a profile that boasts tens of thousands of followers, with posts having an average of hundreds if not dozens of likes, but who am I to tell someone how to scam?

My slickness aside, though, I have not been influenced by Instagram in any of those ways, and my frequent usage hasn't impacted the way I think. That's why as much as I love and enjoy Instagram, there are some parts of it I do not enjoy: how it occasionally makes me feel about myself, for example.

For the most part, I've learned not to allow how other people view me to alter how I view myself. It's easier to stay on top of that task when you're not subjecting yourself to care-fully curated depictions of other people's lives. The longer I use Instagram, the more those images start to seep in.

A slightly older friend of mine once gave me pause as we were discussing my disappointment with the state of my career as compared to select contemporaries of mine. "I don't believe in that," she said of measuring myself against others. "Some-times you actually do need to compare yourself to other people to gauge what you're not doing right." She meant this more in the professional sense, but I had already been doing a less than ideal version of that through my Instagram feed by the time she dropped that spicy nugget.

Overall, if I didn't know any better, I'd say that most of the population aged twenty-five to forty are living their best lives.

They frequently travel to Dubai, Brazil, and Bali. Very few folks still have body fat, thanks to their personal trainer and intermittent fasting conducted while doing Keto or Whole30. Everyone is in designer clothes. Everyone looks like they're having more fun than you when you're not so thrilled about your own affairs.

One doesn't have to be superficial and materialistic to let it get in your head; repetition takes down the mightiest of us.

There are some in particular that have gotten to me.

I can't tell if I'm attracted to him or hate his absolute guts— for reasons that are valid or rooted in envy. I suspect it is some uncomfortable combination of the two. Regardless, I'm tuned in. I can't look away. I watch every single Instastory he puts up as if it's must-see TV even though more often than not it's some goofy bullshit. I check his timeline, too, where he is less frequent in output, but given Instagram's enraging decision to no longer allow our timelines to be dictated chronologically— resulting in me seeing Father's Day–themed posts a week before I have to tip to this Fourth of July turn up—I probably would have missed something anyway. Okay, no I wouldn't have. I check the page too frequently to miss any, uh, content.

My body recoils when considering how pathetic this sounds when laid bare.

He is a particular type of braggart. Once, he posted his salary for the upcoming year. I already figured he made a lot of money. He was constantly posting himself shopping or showing off the aftermath of said shopping. Saint Laurent, Off-White, Gucci, and Thom Browne, among a sea of other high-end labels. His style itself isn't particularly impressive. You can tell he's a bit agnostic when it comes to having an actual aesthetic; he's a label whore, if anything. It doesn't totally cross the line into outright gaudy, but the tip is in.

Not that it matters. It's hard to imagine tact is ever a real point of concern for him. The intent here is to stunt, and in that aim, he is a great success. I would love to know if he at all was influenced by the show *Lifestyles of the Rich and Famous*. His antics remind me of that show. I used to get a kick out of that show. It made you want to be rich. Nothing looked better than being rich. Look at their houses. Look at their clothes. Doesn't that look like the life?

Obviously, there ain't nothing but some white folks before you on the TV screen, but you block it out so your lil' Black ass can dream and be caught up in the fantasy like anyone else watching.

What I didn't know at the time was that as much as I hear pundits (who should be providing the world anything else besides punditry) bark about "class warfare," they don't talk about its true culprits. The criticism of the rich is not rooted in people being successful enough to become wealthy, but a system that allows people to build massive fortunes based on exploitation—and using that power to consolidate power that prevents them from ever facing any consequences for such abuses. The problem isn't whether or not you can afford the yacht you're showing off on television, but whether or not activities like, say, not paying people livable wages are how you were able to pay for that yacht. Or was it being let off the hook for paying your fair share of taxes? Or was it through monopoly-building. Not to sound like I'm a TV character that just enrolled in a prestigious fictitious university where I am newly politicized, but *Lifestyles of the Rich and Famous* was plutocratic propaganda. (Shame on you, Robin Leach!)

Having said all of that, his flaunting is unnecessary, and his literal money brags tacky and not in tune with the times, but I'd still fuck.

As for the other, who I'm even more zoned into, he makes me regret eating solid food for a significant portion of his frequent posts. His posts are somewhat self-aggrandizing, but I suppose Instagram is designed for self-aggrandizement. I guess what ticks me off a little bit is the poorly disguised humility. But not more than the overall corniness. Why can't folks post their thirst traps and let the intended audience salivate in peace?

You can always tell when a person used to feel lame, and following a new body, location, change, career, and so on, they now feel cool and are pressed to prove it. Somehow, that overtime will help offset past droughts. There's something beautiful in someone being able to transform themselves in a way that makes them happy. I'm all for people who can embody the chorus of "Butterfly," one of the trademark songs from the elusive chanteuse Mariah Carey. Spread your wings and shit.

However, people who suffer from the Mike Jones can be nauseating. The line "Back then they didn't want me, now I'm hot, hoes all on me" is a moment to stunt but not a place to permanently reside. He sometimes gives that, and if he hadn't already shared his background with me and suggested he wasn't totally over it, his online antics would have confirmed it all the same.

He's so cute, though. And smart. Cultured, if not "classy." Kind of perfect, if not stubbornly stuck in that period when he didn't get to sit with the cool kids. I'm not now humming "We Shall Overcome"; you are.

On top of it all, he looks like he did everything right. The schools. The line of work. Everything looks so well tailored. I can hear screams telling me to find a better fit for myself already.

As specific as these descriptions might seem, I can guarantee the people who assume I am speaking about them will be wrong and the persons I'm talking about won't have the slightest clue. It truly doesn't matter. I shouldn't be so engulfed in the images of these people anyway, right?

As for why I don't just unfollow, I know them both. Sometimes people take unfollowing as if you challenged them to a duel or called for their permanent exile from your social circle. I don't want to be bothered with the blowback; I mute and boot in most cases, but in these, I can't look away. I can't even try to downplay how odd this sounds by noting that at least each person I mentioned is a person I actually know, but I have kept up with the habits of strangers on the platform, too. After all, so many of the gay boys on the internet look and post the same anyway.

I know I should know better than to let any of this get to me.

The median income in 2017 in the U.S. was $61,372. For Black people, the United States Census Bureau reported the median was $40,258. It was $39,490 for us in 2016, but hold your applause, as it was $41,363 in 2000. Those two folks I described aren't lying about their lives, because I know their jobs, but how are the rest of you people in Fiji? I make more than both medians, but chose the wrong kind of debt. I wish I had chosen more fun ways to owe somebody—like going to Mykonos, for starters.

I know some of these people are flat-out lying about their lives. The perfect couple that became an open relationship to satisfy one person's urges at the expense of the other's feelings. The one that's tens of thousands in debt as a result of their need to present as perfect. The fool who is repurposing someone else's material to the cheers of commenters who won't ever know the con.

Some are not technically lying. The flight attendant who feels the need to boast of being a world traveler—"While you were in bed, I was on a flight to Amsterdam." Yeah, you were at work. You'll be in Des Moines, Iowa, tomorrow. Safe travels.

I don't feign superiority. Many of us are showing the most favorable portrayals of our lives in one capacity or another. I'm no less guilty of this than anyone else. Why would anyone want to advertise what they don't like about themselves? But that emphasis on mainly positive portrayals gives way to us being a big circle jerk of false impressions of our nuanced lives.

Knowing people aren't being totally honest with what they are showing you doesn't mean what they show you still can't get to you. We live in a political climate in which the truth doesn't matter. I suppose it didn't hit me until it was too late that gaslighting may not hit me in some areas but will undoubtedly slap me on the back of my neck in others.

Sometimes I wonder if the images I have shared on my feed might be causing someone else to have similar feelings. Everything looks better on someone else. Sometimes those images did exacerbate stress and anxiety I had over making more money. Sometimes I would go on there looking to feel connected and leave feeling lonelier than before.

My best friend dré (as previously noted in my first book, he prefers a lowercase aesthetic, and friendship is catering to your friends' aesthetic choices in all forms) used to profess his disdain of Instagram. His actual IG handle used to pronounce that contempt.

dré is one of the most impressive people I have ever met and he's a confident person, so I didn't want to believe social media had any impact on him. I didn't want to because I didn't want to acknowledge how influenced I was, too. At least he had the good sense to stay off Instagram.

Years had passed since that conversation. My incredibly smart, charismatic, talented, and skillful friend had become even more impressive in terms of titles and what else comes back with them. It was a by-product of years of hard work yielding just rewards. I asked him about that conversation because I was trying to recall specifics about what he said at the time that I couldn't truly appreciate until later.

"well my thing was always, IG was the greatest hits of everyone's life," dré texted me. "everyone's best angles, everyone's best job moments, everyone's best relationship—and I was in a place where I wasn't 100% comfortable about where I was in life. it wasn't fun/funny/social; it was making me feel insecure about EVERYTHING."

Instagram became more fun for him once he felt better, but it took me a little while longer. Even what constituted better in me made me think it wasn't enough. That's indicative of being an ingrate. I know that everyone's path is different. I understand that what's for one person is for them, and what's yours is yours. But if you go on a platform where everyone's showing their best, it can potentially delude you into thinking nothing you have is good enough. It's similar to what traditional media can do to you. I won't pretend that realization instantly led me to no longer looking at people who appear to be leading better lives with superior bodies and greater disposable income, but I have altered some behavior—starting with electing to spend less time on Instagram.

I used to look backward when bored. I don't know why I'd occasionally go back and look at people I let go of or who threw me back in the water, but I did. There was someone in particular I would revisit more than the others. There was no point to go and look at him stand next to the man he chose over me, the one he didn't want, but I looked for a while. Curiosity should be applied more selectively.

And I've considered spending more useful time in the morning—like looking at amateur porn on Twitter or just catching up on NPR podcasts. And then telling myself what ought to be obvious, but I can be dense. Go back to running my own race. Stop allowing comparison to steal my joy. All that affirmation shit. Whatever it takes.

Because I love Instagram. I want to keep loving Instagram. It's still where all the cute boys are. It's where my people are.

I just have to remember that I'm watching de facto commercials of other people's lives, so view them within reason, and when all else fails, look away. I don't need nobody bringing me no bad news, and I don't need to go looking for reasons to make myself feel bad. And if I can't stop myself from scrolling for too long on a given day, there's now a setting on Instagram for folks whose self-control may fail them on a given day: a timer that alerts you the second you've reached your daily allotted time for Instagram usage that day. Bless my heart.

SWIPE UP

I have never been that fond of porn. The first time I ever shared this fact with someone, I instantly heard the shock and subsequent disappointment in his tone. It recalled the period in my life when I did not eat beef or pork. Whenever I made that admission to a southern Black elder, they would gawk at me and speak to me as if I had let down, if not the entire race, at least the ones that had good enough sense to never turn down some bacon. *Harriet Tubman didn't risk her life trying to help Black people break from bondage for you to only want the pineapple topping of the holiday ham, Uppity Negro* is the sentiment I felt was often intimated but left unsaid. Unsaid because I got tired of trying to explain that if you get turkey bacon made from the thigh, it's not that bad an alternative to real bacon. After they shook their head the third time at what they dismissed as lies and heresies, I'd shift the conversation to the weather or less combative topics such as "When do you think the race war will finally begin?" and "Who made the potato salad?" despite me not enjoying potato salad.

I will never get potato salad. It doesn't matter who made it, Black people. It doesn't sit right with my stomach or spirit.

I treat porn a lot like potato salad: something I understand to be something that I am supposed to enjoy, but can't wrap my taste buds around.

My history with porn began with me first stumbling upon one of those softcore movies on Cinemax. Does that count? They were simulating fucking on television, so it has to count.

My mom had recently gotten cable, following months and months of badgering her to get cable so I could watch *Wrestlemania VIII*. The pay-per-view viewing was a gift since the event was a week before my birthday. We didn't have Cinemax, but as I learned, we were given a trial period for a week.

Everyone was asleep, but I couldn't knock out, so I went into the living room and flipped channels. That's when I saw some white woman in white lingerie moan with her nipples exposed as some man behind her was pulling her slowly back and forth. She did most of the moaning while he made grunting noises. Her performance was much stronger than his. In the background was music playing that I imagine was intended to speak to the sexual eruption on screen, but sounded more like the background of the Sega Genesis game *Ecco the Dolphin*. Madonna's *Erotica* was released the year I saw this on television. The person who edited this movie should have drawn inspiration from that.

Our home was filled to capacity, but no one came in the living room, because I had the volume low and I sat near the speaker part of the television. If memory serves, that TV was a result of the other one abruptly dying on us and my dad being insistent we take someone's hand-me-down rather than go out and buy a new set—to my mother's dismay but eventual shrug 'cause who wants to argue about this since the big-old-ass television is already here now? I recall having to use pliers to turn the volume up and down because the knob was missing on the too-old-for-the-early-1990s telly. They didn't hear any of it, as I had reached for those pliers at a rapid pace once I saw what was going on.

I only watched it for a few minutes longer before turning to something else and deciding to return to bed and give sleep another try. It would be my luck that one of my parents walked in and then, then . . . um, I'm not sure what would have happened. My dad might have been amused more than anything. That wouldn't have been the kind of thing that upset him. My mom might have yanked me up a little bit, but I lean more into her finding a way to make me feel even more embarrassed. I'm glad both were in bed.

I didn't feel much from what I did see. Maybe I was too young to catch on. I knew sex made babies, and I had crushes and whatnot, but I wasn't at the age where my dick wielded greater influence over my urges and viewing habits.

Once my hormones did declare "we're hummin' comin' at 'cha," those new softcore Cinemax flicks one could catch during another one of their preview trials took on new meaning—in theory anyway. I was mostly curious, and to a greater extent, I was trying to force myself to like women.

I could get erect sometimes from watching the women, but there were obvious difficulties and they were not limited to vaginas being the star of each production. On those Cinemax movies, the women were all white. And like white-white. Most of them were blond. As for the men, they all reflected the same genre of white guy: Steve Sanders on the original *90210*. Why not throw in a Dylan or Brandon knockoff? Obviously, adding melanin into the mix would be too audacious, but why not diversify your white guy? (To not totally shame Cinemax for past grievances, I want to share that I enjoyed *Banshee* and recognize that, in 2008, *Zane's Sex Chronicles* debuted on the network.)

When the internet got faster, I tried to search for color on my mama's Packard Bell—and then the Hewlett Packard she got to replace it. Much of what I saw grossed me out. It didn't look at all appealing. All that bad acting. That production value. And what is it with the racist overtones? You can't even try to get a nut without white supremacy tagging itself in?

Assuming maybe I perhaps needed to try the less-is-more approach with pornography, I turned to magazines—i.e., tradition. *Vibe* was inspiring me creatively, so I asked myself whether or not I just needed to see it in print. I discovered *Playboy* at the barbershop. I must admit, the articles were poppin'. And *Smooth* magazine! I once had my best friend Kim buy me a copy of that because Trina and her big ole booty were on the cover. I pretended to truly love that back shot, but in real life, we could only ever be besties—well, so long as she is fine with the idea of me randomly rapping "Da Baddest Bitch" in its entirety. The same goes for *King* magazine. I didn't care about Esther Baxter's tits or Melyssa Ford's ass. If anything, I was mad I couldn't be dancing in the "Freek-A-Leek" video.

"You're gay, you big ass dummy. Go look at some gay shit" is a response I can recall hearing from yet another person perplexed by my lack of interest in porn.

I was always wary of trying to look at gay porn while living in my parents' house. I was good about clearing the history search often, but something about looking up gay porn felt too risky. I almost did once as my mom walked in from work with the food she'd bought after calling us to ask what we wanted to eat—she was rightfully in no mood to cook after another twelve-hour shift at work. It would have been an utter nightmare if she saw me looking at this man's ass that only could turn on people with a Chewbacca kink.

(Please don't take offense to the invocation of Chewbacca, hairy community. I'm one of you, although I tend to shave. Regardless, I am a *Star Wars* fan, and Chewbacca is my dude, so please don't take that descriptor pejoratively. Now, if I said "Sheev Palpatine ass cheeks," be offended.)

At least if I had gotten caught looking at women, my parents might have felt a sigh of relief. I didn't need this smoke. Thankfully she missed me. If I were going to be caught looking at some naked man and find myself drowning in a pool of holy water, it'd have to be a man I felt worth it.

I looked at more gay porn when I was in college, but wasn't particularly impressed with it even with freer access.

Gay porn from the bigger companies manages to be more racist than the straight porn I used to watch and squeal at before clicking out. Most of the Black boys are subservient in their roles regardless of whether they take it or put it in. As for the gay Black gay porn, respectfully, the economic inequality screams at you so much that me, a caring person, cannot watch that and not want to write an essay about inequitable allocation of income and resources—not the kind of hot take that's supposed to be happening in this situation.

After a while, I stopped trying. I chalked it up as somewhat of a personal failure. I'm too picky. I'm prudish. I shouldn't be thinking about trickle down economics while looking at ass cheeks being clapped anyway. I like figuring out new and interesting ways to fault the Catholic Church for something, so I threw that in as an excuse, too. The Pope will deal.

However, I consider myself enlightened now. Much of the credit goes to the thots I follow on Twitter and Instagram who indirectly led me to a revelation that I, too, can enjoy adult entertainment, only with a model that's more peer-to-peer and oddly populist.

OnlyFans is a membership platform that allows "fans" to pay a subscription to see content from "earners." In other words, it's a way for people to sell their nudes directly to the consumer. As a business model, I found it ingenious— particularly for nonwhite queer men.

I became a customer after an extremely long time of internal debate.

I thought I was too good to be spending money on amateur porn. These days, you don't even have to pay for porn. Although I use Twitter mostly to talk politics and reveal what song I am dancing to in the morning, there is a plethora of pornography floating throughout that site. I discovered this going through someone's likes on Twitter. But most of what I saw reminded me of what I hated about porn—the dustiness of some of the participants, the weird racial politics, and the angles I wish were more tailored to my interests.

The earner I chose posted plenty of previews. You could get off from those alone. I don't think a lot of them who have OnlyFans pages grasp that there is enticing people and then there is giving them so much in your preview that it doesn't push people to actually spend their money because you've already satiated their curiosity. He posted too much, but I ended up giving in anyway.

Not with an actual subscription. I was not letting my debit

or credit card bill reflect that. I never wanted to see my loan payments on the same list as my newfound porn habit. This kind soul allowed those who had issues with subscribing on OnlyFans for whatever reason to send him money via Cash App for their thirty-day window.

You don't need to know all he did on his account, but I can confirm being thoroughly entertained. Maybe it was the fact that he looked like someone I could realistically be around if we were located in the same location. Or that he dispelled a lot of the presumptions people make about those who turn to porn—e.g., nothing about him suggested I needed to feel bad. He had agency, so I could enjoy his content without trying to contextualize it. Let the right head guide me, as it were.

I won't say ole boy was the wind beneath my wings, but once I was able to see the content after being granted access, I did hear Bette Midler sing, "Did you ever know that you're my hero?" while watching one post in particular.

I tried to write about OnlyFans for work once. Not solely as a democratization of porn in which those more likely to be marginalized in the porn world have control and a larger private share, but generally, how it's to me like the equivalent of that grocery store Aldi, in that it's without all the bells and whistles but serviceable and cost-effective. It's kind of European to boot, because don't the Euros love a good peep show?

Not to mention, after finding out that some of these extra-fit folks have made thousands of dollars just for showing off their body parts to thirsty men like me, I applauded their hustle.

Consider all of the thirst traps you might see people post on Instagram. Depending on your social circle—and mine consists of lots and lots of queer men—you may see a wave of ass cheeks, toned bodies, and behavior I can only describe as misguided attempts to do seductive karaoke. And depending on some of your friends and what they like on IG, if you turn to your Explore page, there's a whole lot more going on. I don't feel old enough to put into words some of what I've spotted there, and won't feel old enough until my AARP subscription is at least six and a half years old.

It's all there for free.

As much as I've seen people complain about others giving away their creativity on Twitter, I applaud these young men for finding a way to earn a profit off of our collective thirstiness. That's not to say that everything we do must be commodified. If you're a voyeur who doesn't mind spreading wide eagle without compensation, do it and have yourself a great time. On the other hand, I bet most economists would agree with me that showing your ass crack for 107 likes on Instagram is not the shrewdest move to make in this economy. Of that 107, we all know about 12 to 15 of those accounts come from users who are bots that will turn into accounts selling weave or Republican falsehoods before you know it.

Why not if you want to?

Still, I am aware that for some people, this is a bit of a last resort.

As fate would have it, I learned someone that went to my gym had an active account.

His name was Abram. I thought he was a very light-skinned Puerto Rican or Dominican, but it turned out he was Russian. He had a fade and looked "swirly" as my daytime TV deity, Wendy Williams, would say. In my partial defense, I've since learned, while at brunch at a restaurant called the Grange, that a lot of Dominican men are named Vladimir. Our server was Dominican and named Vladimir. Although he did offer some explanation behind that fun fact, I can't remember a single thing he said. However, I can say with complete clarity and conviction that Dominican Vladimir had the kind of smile that makes you swoon internally about the gift of sodomy. Also: that spot really should bring back its biscuit sandwich with fried chicken and sausage gravy.

Abram had a very low haircut and stood out from all of the other white men in the gym who relocated to Harlem and started hogging the squat racks.

By the time I made the connection, my pitch was passed on. As legend has it, my direct editor was heavily into the idea, but her boss apparently didn't want to dissect pornography in his section of the publication. That section did, more than a year later after my initial pitch, but sometimes progress bends to another's byline.

There may have been no point in talking with Abram for journalistic reasons, but I was intrigued for my own reasons, so I wanted to have a conversation regardless. I appreciated OnlyFans helping me once again find pleasure in a way that felt most comfortable to me and all that paranoia about sex that I continued to shake off with time. I was fascinated to know how he felt about what he was doing. Unfortunately, the exchange gave me sad after-school special. What he advertised on Instagram (and Grindr) was nothing compared to how he actually felt about his new line of work.

"It's too hard for me to post something personal like porn on OnlyFans and I'm crying every day about it," Abram told me. "Because my music is not so popular and I do that only for money."

If you looked at Abram, with his chiseled face, abs, tattoos, and body that makes you regret allowing bread into your life, you would assume he made music like Zayn. He was actually a composer and pianist from Moscow.

"I hate this country. First time I came, it was for performance at Carnegie and now I'm posting some porn . . . it's horrible."

It reminded me of a comment a guy made to me while I was prepping my original pitch.

"It's more interesting to me when I see people who resort solely to sexual expression as a means to support themselves," he told me. "Not judging at all, because I'm guilty of indulging, but I just wonder if certain broadcasters are only presenting themselves because they aren't motivated or have limited opportunities to financially pull themselves out of their current situation."

As if I weren't teetering toward flaccid already now, he continued by asking, "Is this form of quick money any better than drug money? At whose expense?"

I appreciated his line of thinking coming from a sincere place of concern and pondering of the larger ramifications of so many young men increasingly turning to pornography. Still, like, can I just enjoy my new favorite toy in peace? I need dumber friends.

Now, I believe it's perfectly reasonable to highlight that this line of work is not an ideal circumstance for everyone, much less their first choice, but as someone who grew up around people who sold drugs, I can tell you that those people were largely glamorized. I won't lump those selling dime bags, but for those who sold harder drugs, they were poisoning people for their own survival, whereas people who provide sex work are often dehumanized, and their contributions trivialized.

And contribution is not a misnomer. For the guy with the

OnlyFans account who got me to put some money in his collection plate provided a service, and based on his responses and posts, he appreciated the transaction. As long as he and others enjoy what they do and figure out that looming tax bill awaiting them, I don't want to assign too much blame to them.

I did feel bad for Abram, though.

I never subscribed to his OnlyFans, but I found one of his EPs on iTunes and bought it. I don't know how to properly describe his music, but it is great music to smoke weed and chill the fuck out already to. And clean. And write. And read. All that classy shit. Way to go, Abram.

We had another exchange via WhatsApp. When I asked if he enjoyed what he did at all, he told me "a little bit," but said he was stopping soon because he was in a relationship. I wanted to tell him "Bust down, Russiana," but I realized (1) he wouldn't get the reference, and (2) it was wildly inappropriate of me. So instead, I told him that after listening to his music, I thought that his talent was bigger than whatever doubts he had about what he was doing in the meantime.

"Thank you. I know that. But the real world is different, anybody needs cock/ass pics, not music."

I told him that he needed to listen to more contemporary music. He said I was funny and soon after asked a question that I gathered translated well regardless of background: "WYD?"

For a dude that grew up paranoid about sex and nearly ruined by prudishness, the prospect of fucking an incredibly handsome, fit Russian who dabbled in amateur porn was appealing. Not only would it feel triumphant for obvious reasons, it also sounds like the synopsis of an independent film that becomes Oscar bait after the Kremlin bans it in Russia. I didn't go that night. Or the other two times he hit me up after. I made up excuses.

He had a boyfriend! I didn't need the guilt. Looking back, I know that's good karma and all, but I regret having to tell that Russian "NO COLLUSION!"

Last I heard, he had moved to Los Angeles, so he's either going to get back to his music, dance as a go-go boy in WeHo, or end up on reality television—maybe all of the above if he really pushes himself. He took all of his OnlyFans-related material down.

God, I wish I had fucked him.

As for the one who got me to pay mind and money to OnlyFans, he's upped his production values and posts of designer *tings*. Good for him. And good for me. I'm supporting the arts!

Through him, I finally understand what the rest of you perverts have gotten out of porn all this time. I simply had a more artisanal flair for it. He and his page showed me the way. All I had to do was stop playing and swipe up.

I feel so much closer to you porn people now. To not tip your porn star is arguably even less civilized than not tipping at a restaurant.

Please support the arts.

IT'S CHEAPER TO DIE

I was not raised to be one of those Black men who avoid the doctor at all costs. My mama, a nurse, made certain that whatever the health care equivalent of "nails done, hair done, everything did" was, we had it.

I remember all of the doctors I came across growing up. Dr. Stevens looked like all of the light-skinned women who were releasing R&B albums around the time: Vanessa Williams, Jasmine Guy, Tisha Campbell, Pebbles, and other Lite Brites serving you several eight-counts in tights. She had recently moved from Chicago, and I was one of her first new patients. I used to repeatedly have extremely painful cases of strep throat. Dr. Stevens had a soothing voice—helpful in assuaging the fears of a kid about to have his tonsils removed. I was six when it happened, so my memory of the operation itself is a bit shaky: I remember lying on my back on a gurney at St. Joseph's Hospital and an anesthesiologist explaining to me that as soon as that mask went over my nose, I should start counting to ten. After waking up, I was told that everything went fine and I would have less pain moving forward. Before going home I was reminded by both her and my mom not to eat anything like a Chicken Nugget in the first couple of days after the operation. I did so anyway. It hurt so bad when I reached into my brother's food, grabbed that Nugget, dipped it in sweet-and-sour sauce, and inhaled it. The skin on a McDonald's Chicken Nugget can occasionally be sharp enough to slash someone's tires. I deserved what I got for not following instructions, but there's only so much Blue Bell and soup a child can stand in such a short amount of time.

Dr. Michaels reminded me of the late comedian Robin Harris because he talked like the dad in *Bébé's Kids*, which Harris created. In the face, he was more so a heavy-set Bernie Mac. He used to lean in the chair at his office like all of the Black dudes who played dominoes outside with my pops. That or any Black man driving a Cadillac Eldorado fresh off of a wash and wax. Rest in peace, icon.

After watching multiple seasons of Bravo's greatest creation, *Married to Medicine*, I'd be remiss if I overlooked my tooth cleaners and smile shapers. I don't want to further insult the work of Dr. Heavenly and others. All I can recall about Dr. Richards, the dentist, though, was that he used to be at an office in our hood until he suddenly moved closer to a location by what was then known as the Summit, before it became the Compaq Center, and eventually Joel Osteen's Lakewood Church. Oh, he had a weird smile, too. My mom never liked him and later explained that he was a (Black) Scientologist, which, in her mind, explained the oddity of his grin and the root of her disdain. Not into the idea of mixing Dianetics with dentistry, we stopped going there after a while, and much of my dental work over the years has been negated by my breaking my retainer and my wisdom teeth coming in, but eventually, I'll make my way to the Smile Store. My teeth are white, but crooked. My friend Nnete once said they had "personality." That's generous, but while I can't afford whatever teeth T.I. has purchased with his health, I consider them a template on what to shoot for when I get a remix on this mouth of mine.

By high school, I had my first white doctor: Dr. B. I forget his surname as he insisted on being identified as Dr. B. He was genial as fuck. And he took an actual interest in me that never felt like pandering. I knew just enough to feign interest in talking sports with him outside of which professional athletes I fantasized about, but what built our rapport more was my interest in news and politics and a vision of what I hoped my professional life might look like. To this day, he asks my mom about me—mostly if I'm still writing.

The names of all of the specialists escape me, but I saw plenty well before high school ended. Of the various problems, the one constant involved my ears—I have been told repeatedly that I have an incredibly thin ear canal. As a result of that, every few years, I get an excruciatingly painful ear infection that always-always-always forces me to take a trip to an ear/nose/throat doctor. Around sixteen or so, I was required to have some operation that sought to remove ear wax stuck to some kind of bone in my ear. I swear I am not a dirty, dusty peasant. I also know that Q-tips only worsen such a situation. It's not that I am forgetting to wash every part of my body. I'm not—never mind. I have a condition! I can't help the ear canals I was born with the same way I can't alter the fact that my ears in general are slightly too big for my peanut head.

But even when I was disgusting myself while seeking medical care, I always had a relatively good experience with doctors.

I had no reason to fear them. I never had an anxiety about a doctor's trip, given that it had been my experience that if something went wrong, it would get taken care of. It might hurt like hell along the way, but eventually, I'd be all right. I just needed to make sure to go when a situation called for it.

We may have wanted for some things, but not our health.

My mom had good insurance, but in recalling all of the doctor's visits through the years, I imagine that if her health insurance had not been so good, I would have been an even more expensive little problem. My mom changed her insurance by the time I graduated from college, in order for me to stay on her plan until I was twenty-five. She knew her sick-ass child might need it.

When the plan told my Black ass I had to go and get my own, it took less than a month of me not on my mom's insurance plan to get another ear infection—one that didn't bother with pretense and so jumped ahead of mild and rushed instantly to wildly painful and frustrating. There is no pain like ear canal pain, beloveds. I wouldn't wish that on anyone. The free clinic made the problem worse—I couldn't hear out of the right side of my head anymore, but outside of the near two days it took to be treated in the emergency room and almost having to run over some bad-ass kids who circled my car while I applied for health insurance, it could have been much worse. (Don't feel bad for those kids either; rob niggas your own age.)

For the first few years of having insurance on my own, while I had to work through my learning curve to avoid racist and/or homophobic doctors, I was good about taking care of myself. The weird things happening with my skin; the unbearable headaches; my ears, again; what I came to learn was a panic attack. The low cost of those generic forms of antidepressants in particular saved my life in one form or another.

I was one of the apparent few millennials who purchased health care plans pre-Obamacare. It wasn't only an earache that pushed me back to insurance. It was knowing its value to begin with from the values my mom the nurse instilled in me. I also never got over Big Mama losing her leg in *Soul Food* and those niggas going back to eating the exact foods that took her ass out of the game.

I had more direct examples to turn to as well.

Joshua was one of the few male friends I had in my teens. Not just cool with—I was cool with plenty of people—but an actual friend. I was sociable, but considered "soft" by a lot of people. That wasn't the easiest way to make male friends—who could sniff out what I was trying to suppress—but Joshua was my friend. He was a football player and ran track, but he was smart and we found each other amusing. He also seemed to have a lot of secrets. Once, he and I along with maybe seven others took a bus trip to visit one of the bigger universities in Texas our senior year. We had to meet at 5 a.m. because it was going to take nine hours to get to our destination. It gave teases of "Welcome to our Very White Campus, Urban Youths." Joshua ended up at the school based on that visit, but by the time we got back to Houston—it had to have been at least 10 p.m.—everyone walked to their parents meeting the bus except him. No one had shown up for Joshua. My mom noticed it faster than I did and we decided to wait with him a little longer. We ended up taking him home. There was someone back at the house, but he never told me why no one was there to pick him up and take him home. He had only made mild allusions to discomfort with his mom, but nothing specific. I wasn't volunteering information about my home life, so I didn't pry.

We kept in touch for a good while—instant messenger conversations, email, and Facebook here and there. He paid a surprise visit to my house on Thanksgiving one year to see me, but I wasn't home yet. I told him that he should have hit me up! I was going to be there in a few days. He would be gone by then, going with his family somewhere else. I was bummed that I had missed him. I had no idea that was going to be the last chance I ever had to see his face and hear his voice—slightly deep and always in a tone best described as "chill." He was a lot calmer than I ever was, but he was funny himself on the low-low.

I don't know if he ever really liked dudes, too, as a few others hinted by the time we both were in college. I heard he was spotted at a gay club in Houston. That didn't necessarily mean he was gay. He was the kind of person who might have popped up there to be supportive. He was considerate in that way. He was attractive, and I can admit looking at him in that way from time to time, but I never gave him any indication. I talked to him about girls. I even tried to hook him up with one of my friends around the time we first became closer. I was more into having a platonic relationship with another dude in which I didn't feel like I had to tone down any parts of myself that I guess screamed "gay," in order to be considered "normal" enough for another dude to be my friend and not assume that anything he assumed about me suggested anything about him. If he ever did have any discomfort when we hung out, he never made it known to me.

We lost touch in the last two and a half years he was alive. I found out through mutual friends that he was experiencing some sudden health problems—something about the liver, I think—and was rapidly declining in health. He didn't have insurance. Then people were trying to raise money on Facebook. This was long before the days of crowdsourcing's peak. He died at a county hospital a few months after he had literally just gotten an advanced degree. He had had his entire life ahead of him and he died at the very start of his late twenties. I was nowhere near Houston when it happened. I wish I had asked my mom to help me fly down to say goodbye properly. To say thank you for being a friend and then proceed to sing the rest of the *Golden Girls* theme because you can't say the words "thank you for being a friend" and not finish the rest of the song—no matter the situation.

He wasn't the first childhood friend of mine to die too soon, but he was the first I knew who might not have had to die if only he'd had access to health care sooner.

I thought of him when the Affordable Care Act gained congressional approval, given that he died only about four months later. I was sad about him, but happy about the bill itself. The only people who weren't happy about the legislation were monsters—the types of people who enjoyed watching Scar murder his brother Mufasa. More people deserved health insurance—especially those who had been robbed of it for preexisting conditions.

Still, I have a secret: Obamacare has since become the bane of my existence and the reason I have become that Black fool who avoids going to the doctor at all costs. I never wanted to be that Black man. There are so many ways to die early as hell as a Black man, and not being the Black man who gets a regular checkup ranks right up there with "just being a Black man in America."

The conservative media industrial complex has already taken that declaration and plastered it on television. I can see the chyron on *Tucker Carlson Tonight* now: "NEGRO AND HOMO WRITER HATES SOCIALIST HEALTH CARE PLAN CRAFTED BY FELLOW DARKIE!"

I take no pleasure in sharing this. I would never want to intentionally upset my beloved Michelle Obama, the greatest First Lady this racist-ass country has ever had. Nor do I want to disappoint Sasha or Malia Obama, as I am sure one of them will at least have a dope podcast that I would die to appear on. And you know, Barry, too. I don't want to shit on the biggest legislative achievement of not only the first Black president of the United States of America, but the greatest legislative win for Democrats in decades.

I've got to two-step in my truth, though. Obamacare has made it harder for me to not end up having a future bout with gout. I am not a selfish person. I understand that Obamacare needed to happen because for far too long, millions of people who needed health insurance were denied that right, long treated as a privilege. I recognize that the problems with the ACA are not totally former President Obama's fault.

In December 2009, Senator Joe Lieberman, no longer a Democrat in name upon losing a 2006 primary to Ned Lamont, only to run as an independent and be reelected as senator of Connecticut, told the Senate majority leader, Harry Reid, to scrap the idea of expanding Medicare and abandon any new government insurance or lose his vote. Democrats in the Senate had previously believed they had Lieberman's support, but being the hating-ass bitch he is, Lieberman flip-flopped.

On his decision, Lieberman said during an appearance on

CBS's *Face the Nation*: "You've got to take out the Medicare buy-in. You've got to forget about the public option."

He claimed it was about concerns over deficits, but it felt more like a personal *fuck you* to Obama and a Democratic Party that no longer catered to him until he held their health care bill for ransom. They acquiesced. Ultimately, the bill was named after former President Obama, and neither he nor any of the Democrats pushed hard enough to pass a bill that Republicans were never planning to support anyway, despite the delightful irony that Obamacare is just Romneycare, which is just Bob Dole's health care plan from the 1990s. So I place most of my contempt where it belongs, but it should be spread around a bit.

It was Obama himself who said on July 18, 2009: "Any plan I sign must include an insurance exchange—a one-stop-shopping marketplace where you can compare the benefits, costs and track records of a variety of plans, including a public option to increase competition and keep insurance companies honest."

As an independent contractor, I am responsible for my health insurance bill. Some boast about the rise of the gig economy and some berate those working nine to five to make a living rather than being an entrepreneur. Let me tell you, I envy you W-2 bitches. You don't have my tax headaches, and more importantly, you generally have health care provided by your employer. I would be less envious if my options were better.

Initially, Obamacare had no real impact on me in terms of what I paid for my insurance. The good old days, as I've now come to see them. My plan stayed roughly in the $170 to $200 per month range and I was free to make the most of my PPO.

Three years in, my very reasonably priced plan rapidly surged in price as some had warned it would without a public option to compete with the private sector. Even after I paid the new higher premium, I would be informed by fall that the plan I had would no longer be available in the next enrollment year. Because my insurance company was leaving the market. So I had to join another. And then they left, so I had to find some new folks.

I miss Aetna so much. That was my bitch until she decided she couldn't be bothered with the Obamacare market anymore. Once, I called a different health insurance provider for information about their plan and she said that for well over $400 per month, I could basically get a physical a year and one trip to the emergency room. It was the third year I lived in New York, and I was trying to find a plan comparable to the ones I'd enjoyed in California and Texas. Everything is more expensive in New York, but when she told me that price, I literally laughed out loud and hung up. More of the markets have left, and my current provider is basically that bae that let themselves go and always wants to punish me for every wrong that I've ever done in life.

What I have settled on now is mostly insurance by name alone. For around $350, I have a shitty HMO that doesn't give me much in the way of options of doctors; the visits cost far more than they should, the deductible is too high, and the drugs that used to be cheap for me are no longer covered. God forbid I get cancer, but if that were to happen—it's surely happened to enough people in my age group at this point—I would basically take that garbage insurance and use it to access doctors in the Texas Medical Center, where you would want to be if the worst should happen. I will turn to GoFundMe to cover the rest—like so many others. I am not being facetious. It's the best I can do for right now until I meet the requirements to join a union that would provide insurance. Or marry someone—preferably in the military. I'd say a rapper, but a lot of them don't have health insurance at all.

When I've tried to explain my situation in the past, many have barked back something about the subsidies associated with Obamacare. Yeah, about that: If you make even 3 cents over the median U.S. income, ya ain't getting naan subsidy. Guess who makes way more than the subsidies but doesn't make nearly enough to afford these ridiculous private health insurance plans plus my private student loans, credit card debt, rent, cable, internet, and free condoms they hand out every Pride?

A public option would have at least provided an opportunity for better for less. Joe Lieberman isn't dead yet, but I hope someone taps me to write his obituary. I'll praise his speaking voice for its "White Barry White" teases, but his vindictiveness and poor judgment will catch these words.

Like any aging person, my body has turned on me.

My stomach truly antagonizes the everlasting hell out of me. Do I have IBS? Or is it the copious amounts of caffeine I drink all day, every day, in order to work obsessively to cover my ass (barely) and not turn into a blob of a man? I made the mistake of going to WebMD to see what my symptoms suggested. At last count, I believe I died four years ago. Everyone can appreciate a strong digestive system, but not one that acts like it's on speed. I don't even like hearing about gas much less bowel movements, but this shit can derail my day and I want to scream for a solution.

Not often but sometimes, there is a pain. Whenever it gets too unbearable, I go to urgent care. That's pretty much my health care now: When something gets too unbearable for my high threshold of pain, I go to urgent care, and complain about the bill months later because it wasn't so expensive only a few years ago.

The last time I went to urgent care, the doctor tried to diagnosis me with syphilis. I don't know if there was a language barrier—perhaps my country twang was too much for this Black woman who spoke like Gabrielle Union doing an impersonation of Lindsay Lohan's weird British accent—but I told her that no, a dick had not been inside me recently. I didn't want to get into sexual politics, just for her to tell me what the lick reads on this pain.

For the life of me, I will never get why some doctors want me to have syphilis so much. This had already happened several years before in Los Angeles. Now, in Harlem, Dr. Girl, I Hate You is trying to once again give me this diagnosis, despite me explaining to her that I have not been in anything lately and nothing has been in me. She prescribed some medicine that my latest terrible insurance plan didn't cover, but the state had some discount program for one of the drugs in particular—it was expensive with the discount, but much worse without. I should call the medical board. I still don't know the root of my gastrointestinal problems, but I know if I die like Elvis Presley, I will return as a ghost and haunt a lot of pawns of the health insurance industry. I hope loperamide abuse isn't a major health concern.

And oh bitch, do I have arthritis already? These long-ass arms have been folded up like a Tyrannosaurus rex's for a decade in my work for the content factory, and they are finding new and interesting ways of pushing me toward greater consideration of writing by way of voice notes and dictation.

In the midst of all of this, I try to lead what I consider to be a holistic approach in the wake of my health insurance woes.

I try to eat healthy or healthy-enough most of the time. I repeat the following prayer as I season my food: "Please don't get hypertension! Please don't get hypertension!" I can't be getting strokes and heart attacks. I can't be getting the sugar either, so I try to drink my alcohol straight.

Meanwhile, I don't get as low when I dance as I used to. My friend Maiya once said, "It will be a sad day when Mike doesn't get low anymore, because that'll mean we're getting old." I tell people that I no longer dance like a stripper trying to cover rent for three people, because I am a classy author now. That's true to an extent, but I also saw what happened when Janet Jackson and Britney Spears both hurt their knees. Janet has managed to recuperate over the years, but even she knows when to fall back and let the younger dancers carry her legendary weight. I can still get low, but I haven't done yoga enough to really drop it with confidence. As much as I aspire to be able to dance like Jennifer Lopez in the second half of life, one false pop and drop and I could end up with a walker. It's not worth the risk right now.

I no longer let my friends back home take me anywhere that might end in me running from gunshots. Thankfully, I do enough cardio to be able to run from gunshots, but better safe than sorry. You can get shot anywhere in America, though, so I may have to stop going outside altogether soon.

I am not the only one taking precautions to prevent as much peril as possible.

A writer friend of mine told me she employs a similar strategy. "I ask God to protect my arm every time I cook mac and cheese," she said. But she is dealing with far more serious consequences with her health. "My mama still asking what meds I'm taking to manage lupus and I laugh and tell her to get Twinkie and Dorinda Clark every time."

She once asked if I play "Pray You Catch Me" whenever I season my chicken with Tony Chachere's. I like Tony Chachere's, but I can feel my heart wobbling to Big Freedia whenever I use it, so we've had to have a conscious uncoupling. I have not broken it off completely with Popeyes. Spicy chicken strips are my sanctuary, but I gotta go, I gotta leave. It's not them. It's me.

This is all as hilarious as it is pitiful. We do our best.

I remember one of the last doctors I saw regularly, Dr. Choi, warning me that my stress and depression often sounded like they were the root of many of my problems. She suggested therapy. I told her I would do that when I could afford it and asked for my generic prescription of Celexa in the meanwhile. As much as I would love to address past trauma with a medical professional, my goal in the interim is to stay relatively healthy and, more than anything, functional.

I am fully aware that therapy would benefit me, but I tried to get therapy way back when I was nineteen or twenty. I asked my mom if she could help me find a person to talk to about some of my problems. The person I met was a white guy that was dismissive. I wasn't sure if it was because I didn't explain myself well enough or what. In hindsight, his dismissal of me and the concerns I had about myself—the depression, the highs and lows, etc.—could be attributed to him presumably not knowing what to do with some lanky Black kid trying to explain that he wrestles with the occasional uncontrollable and uncontainable sadness even when he has a smile on his face—like the day he met him.

I do wonder what might have happened had he listened to me. I think the same about Dr. Choi. I didn't know a lot about PrEP, but I was curious about a drug that might be able to protect me from HIV infection. As someone who grew up fearing

AIDS, of course I felt it a good idea to ask about it. She asked me a few questions and ruled that based on my responses, I wasn't an ideal candidate. I guess I wasn't fucking enough at the time. But as someone Black and interested in men sexually, aren't I "high risk" by default?

I bet my insurance didn't cover it anyway, and the drug remains far too expensive to be accessible. The average cost of PrEP is $1,989.57 per month. It's cheaper to die, no? During his second State of the Union Address, Donald Trump announced his plan to end the HIV epidemic by 2030—making PrEP part of that strategy. Yet it costs too much, and on top of that, Republicans continue to make it their goal to undermine if not flat-out dismantle the already imperfect Affordable Care Act, with no real alternative or plan to replace it with.

So the same way I pray over my food as I season it, I say a silent prayer before I . . . enjoy an edible arrangement. And protection. But prayer on top of protection.

Dr. Choi was the last decent doctor I had. My insurance changed and she only took certain kinds—which I increasingly had less ability to pay for. She was the beginning of my reckoning with the reality that even as my insurance becomes much more expensive, the coverage will grow poorer.

Twice I've lost my health insurance over simply not being able to pay for it. I've had to make the choice to default on my loans or be late for the second month of my insurance, which would effectively lead to its cancellation.

The second time was the same week I became a *New York Times* bestselling author. In the next enrollment year, I got another shitty health insurance plan in name only. Maybe that bestselling author part will help generate publicity for the Go-FundMe campaign should I need it. I am confident it may not go that way for me, but you never know. I worry about the others in similar situations or worse anyway.

I stopped going regularly to the doctor around thirty. It's literally just the urgent care if need be and back to Houston if God forbid. I truly did not want to become like all those Black men who just drop dead at forty or fifty or sixty over something even semiregular checkups could have prevented. But I am now that cliché.

Blame Joe Lieberman. Blame the Democrats. Blame the Republicans. Blame the health insurance companies. Blame the lobbyists. Blame the media ghouls who serve propaganda on their behalf. Blame them all. I do, especially whenever I feel permanently attached to a toilet.

In short: Consider all of this an endorsement of universal health care—namely Medicare for All.

SHRINKAGE

I try to remember that no matter what, I am a bad bitch, but every so often I can be worn down to the point where I momentarily conclude otherwise. A tragedy, a parody, but such is life when burdened by not having access to a tech CEO bro's pin number. I am usually able to shake the doubt off fairly fast, but the older I was getting, the more frequently I questioned my place in life and how my future might be shaping up. I was less certain than I had been in years past.

So I don't think it was in my best interest to be sitting in front of someone who I saw as a reflection of everything I was not. It was not his fault he was so amazing and I felt less than stellar. Being up close to him was giving my insecurities an adrenaline rush, but I didn't want to look away and never turned down the invitation to meet up. No matter how he was making me feel on the inside, he was so nice to look at and speak with.

First, Chance, not the rapper, triggered my body dysmorphia. Based on the way his clothes fit his body, he looked as if he had been built in a CrossFit studio before being passed to nonstop SoulCycle classes until he finally got a break to allow Whole30 to further tailor his physique. That immediately let me know how disciplined he was and how undisciplined I was. I go to the gym a lot, but my dieting is mixed. I know how to diet like an Instagram model, but I also sometimes fall into the habits of all those southern Black folks actively courting eventual disaster. You could tell he was not an emotional eater. I bet he only ate turkey burgers and lettuce throughout the week, as opposed to convincing himself that it was okay to have another cookie because they were marked as protein cookies.

His lack of physical flaws did not bother me as much as it might have in the past. Sure, if I ever took my clothes off in front of him, I would have made certain to have done five thousand push-ups prior to showing up, while regretting every carbohydrate I had ever consumed the very second I saw him shirtless, but was I going to turn down the invitation to be in *that* setting? I was not that stupid. He was too fine to be caught up in the rapture of my physical hang-ups. Besides, it'd go the same way it had with the other hurly-burly men I'd met along the way: We'd finish.

One day I'll get the shackles of my back fat removed so I can dance (shirtless). I can already feel Satan's grip tightening around my neck for that sentence, though. Ah, well.

I thought he was a lot smarter than I was, too. He didn't agree with me when I declared such, or if nothing else, wouldn't allow me to actually highlight that tidbit out loud, but all of us can be idiots sometimes. I gathered it was a modesty thing for him. He was very big on presenting modesty. I think it was the southerner in him. I love all men, but there is something special about southern boys to other southern boys. No matter the reason, he was smarter than I was and I didn't mind it at all. I could learn from him. That's not to say I was suddenly the Tomi Lahren to his Rachel Maddow, but he was well read and well educated and thoughtful in ways I hadn't come across in most men—none that looked like him, that's for sure. (For reference's sake, if I were an MSNBC prime-time anchor, I would be Lawrence O'Donnell, who is me if I were an older white man from Boston.)

He liked to debate. A whole lot. I wasn't certain on that conclusion initially—maybe both of us were just too vocal about our differences of opinion? But no, he liked to go back and forth. I don't mind disagreeing with someone and hearing them out, so I suppose debates are fine, although I'd much rather not. He was more into mental jousting than I ever was. People assume that given my line of work, I must love dialogue and debate. I wish people wouldn't assume that. I consume too many thoughts as it is, being on the internet so much as my work dictates. I can go on with life just fine without people wanting to have a hot take off with me at happy hour for sport.

Chance riled me up whenever there was a difference between us, but I enjoyed being challenged by him. He was never provocative for the sake of—always careful with his words. I don't think he necessarily ever needed to be right; he was adamant about a person proving their point, if anything. Whether or not too adamant can remain up for debate, but he was ultimately cerebral in the way my friends always said I needed. He kept me on my toes. I'd like to believe I only offer informed opinions, but there is a tendency for me to be instantaneous in my responses. He forced me to give myself a seven-second delay at times.

He was a lil' classy nigga, to boot. Classy in the way my not at all refined self could benefit from. But he had plenty of low-brow moments in him; he was not pretentious in nature. I need someone who may no longer be invested in *Basketball Wives*, but isn't someone that would shame me for watching that and opting out of *The Handmaid's Tale* after a while—everything about it is so well done, but it can make for such gruesome viewing.

If none of his other positive attributes was convincing enough, I was able to confirm he was it when he ordered a tequila with soda and chicken wings. That is me in an order. If a Nancy Meyers romantic comedy were ever modeled after us, this revelation would be the point in the film where it was clear that one of us needed to let Keanu Reeves go so true love could be enjoyed—blasphemous as that sounds.

He was pretty much my ideal guy. He was handsome; he was brilliant; he was southern; he was thicc; he was Black; his sex was amazing; he was funny albeit in his corny way. He made me want to improve. He was the first person I had met in a long time that I wanted to like me. I think he was into the idea of liking me. This should have gone better than it did in real time.

At this point in my life, I wasn't the paranoid formerly in denial gay trying to figure out if I wanted to step out and be the person I was rather than chasing the one others preferred me to be. I'd figured it out. It was okay to revel in pleasure. God didn't hate me. My mom would not be joining me at the Pride parade for reasons besides the fact that neither of us is big on crowds, but we were talking regularly. I was at as much peace with all of that as I could be. I wanted to move on. To the next stages of life. I wanted a fuller life. I've said this so many times. I needed action.

So here was someone I liked. What do you do when you like someone? You tell them. You make an effort. You do so with the hope they'll like you back. I'm not always the best at this, but I've learned to be fairly efficient at it.

Yet I choked every single time in front of this dude. Not once, not twice, every single time. I bet he'd say otherwise, but he's nice that way. I needed to be Ariana Grande and I was Ashanti. Ashanti is cool—she has hits—and she hits her notes (but should never do so while scooting across the stage by her ass cheeks as seen on the second daytime series hosted by Queen Latifah), but I'm supposed to be shooting for the Mariah Carey–like high note, not the sweet whispers of "Foolish," having people shout "Oh, this used to be my shit" at a thirty-somethings crab boil.

It's not like we weren't enjoying each other's company. He said he was enjoying his time with me. I'm a good time. But I would freeze with him too many times. And when I did speak, he was engaged, though I could sometimes feel myself shrinking.

I liked him, but he was increasingly triggering.

I was grappling with how my life was and the way I preferred it to be. As the saying goes, you mess up and sacrifice in your twenties and everything works out perfectly in your thirties. That's not the exact phrasing. I'm even messing that up. Point is, you should be better put together by a certain age—so I've heard.

I don't want to say I've wasted the third decade of my life. I won't diminish myself in such fashion. I have done many things I am proud of. Things will improve. Some things have already improved. But what hasn't changed is one fundamental fact: so much of my life is still revolving around the $1,000+ a month

I give to my student loan lenders. So much of that money could've gone elsewhere. An IRA account. Better insurance. A house. Actual vacations. Stuff that would make me happy. Projects that creatively would make me feel fulfilled and would more than likely have me already in that better position in life.

And you already know that some of the things other people have that you don't—marriage, home ownership, children— aren't even necessarily things you want right and may never want. Also: Some of your friends have these things and none made their lives happier, much less complete.

You also know that your thirties are not that late in your life. However, in terms of earning potential, career advancement, and compatibility, based on some very adult aspects of life—credit, debt, general stability—this period is pivotal. I've seen people in my line of work who never quite got over the hump. I know people my age who already have. I feel for the former, but I need to be the latter.

My greatest fear is that I won't, and if I don't, what that means.

There are many days in which I wrestle with the guilt of getting out of my hood only to subject myself to more struggle pursuing a dream my kind typically cannot afford to have.

Chance had nothing to do with any this, but in hearing more of his story, I heard the key parts where ours aligned and where they differed. He chose a more stable route to improve his life and I went with something risky. And harder. My career has largely consisted of self-employment and self-teaching on how to not just survive in pursuit of something, but thrive. His was a much clearer path—he understood exactly what results his hard work would yield. That made his debt irksome, but not debilitating. Mine had me both thriving and barely surviving at the same time. I didn't know what to think about myself based on my own metrics, so it was ill-advised to measure myself by his.

He just made me feel like such a broke nigga by comparison. I have listened to too many R&B songs in my life not to know you don't want to be that person. Do you remember the first R&B song that warned you of the futility of the broke nigga?

For me, it was "Tell Me (I'll Be Around)," released in 1996 from the obscure R&B girl group named Shades. On the song, one of them—I don't remember names or faces much—sings, "Don't think that I'm an opportunist, I fall in love, but just not for free." I tried looking this up, so I do know it was not Shannon Walker Williams, the one who married Ray Allen, and thus stayed very true to her mission of marrying a baller. It doesn't look like it was the member named Tiffanie Cardwell, so it was either Danielle Andrews or Monique Peoples. My apologies to the group members, but at least I bought the CD single. Point is, the song was basically cluck-cluck, I need a man with the big bucks. The chorus is truly a gorgeously sung gold digger questionnaire: "Tell me your name, what car do you drive? How much money do you make?"

If Chance and I had to answer this song that I still listen to regularly because the shit still slaps, he would nail all of the questions. I would be asking if my answers could be written. And sorry, but I have been impacted more by the bevy of Kandi Burruss–penned "this broke man ain't shit"–themed tunes so many artists were singing in the aughts than I ever realized. We need to make more economically realistic R&B.

Right before Chance, I made the mistake of going out with someone else that was basically a walking City Girls track. This boy was younger than me and not necessarily dumb per se, but not someone that you could have a conversation with if the topics at hand deviated to anything that involved the world around us versus the world viewed through your social media feeds. He talked a lot about nothing, I looked at him and wrestled with whether he was that pretty or I was this shallow. I like to think if you invite someone out, you should pay for dinner or whatever else is the date. I think it's more than fine to pay for multiple dates if you so desire. Back when I was trying to impress girls in vain, I did the most with the money I made from working. I tried to do that initially when I switched to boys, but I quickly dropped that act because men aren't worth it. And with men, why would we even go by straight people? They don't know anything. Look at them.

This dude was more into tradition. Even when he would invite me out, I would pay. He only once made mention that I always paid, before ordering another drink. I had to cut that one loose. He made too many jokes about escorting anyway— and not the kind I make because it's too late for me now. If he were an escort, I wish he would have at least said his price and I could have made an evaluation yay or nay.

Right before him was Aaron, who I'm convinced believes living as close to Nene Leakes's "I'M VERY RICH" essence is the key to a happy life.

I don't have a problem with people of meager means who go on to make a nice life for themselves, reaping the rewards of their hard-earned success, but new money types are the most insufferable people on the planet. I don't care about which gym you go to. I don't care what class your flight was—though now that you mention it, even comfort seats are amazing for the free liquor and leg room so shout-out to first class, Still, yo chill. I don't care about the car you drive, either.

I don't care not because I don't have those things, but because I'm not sure I even want much of that. My ideal is a quieter stunt and less-is-more approach to showing off whatever constitutes success to you. I think his choices are fine given they are his to make, but they were too loud for me.

Those last two wastes of my time, coupled with my own penchant for self-sabotaging, impacted how I acted with Chance. I could feel myself increasingly shrinking in front of him. Instead of me admitting those issues to myself in an effort to address them, I chose to create reasons not to like him. None of them is worth repeating because none of them made any sense. It was easier to come up with new and varied excuses to dislike him. I'm good at coming up with reasons to push myself away from people. It's far less laborious than admitting my own insecurities.

What I should have done is look myself in the mirror and admit that my own hang-ups about my place in life were why I was failing to impress someone who was steadily losing interest in me. I regret giving him all the reasons to. It was only a temporary feeling.

I can credibly blame my childhood for my delayed start in a romantic and sexual life, but it is my own fault at this point for tripping up my own progress. I am not a failure, but if I don't accept it, I will only continue to fail myself and be rewarded with a dusty dick and hurt feelings.

I don't know where the intersection of Suze Orman and Iyanla Vanzant is, but there is a market for that.

Although I blew it with that beautiful, well-off gym rat who debated like a prosecutor seeking public office, I did reach out to him every now and then to see how he was doing. Eventually, I built up enough nerve to ask him to hang out again.

He had left his high-paying job for something not as well paid but more fulfilling. I confessed that part of my admitted nervousness around him was rooted in him triggering some of my insecurities. I told him how much he intimidated me because of where my head was. In getting to know him, I realized he was a beautiful, thoughtful writer, and because he was so brilliant and thoughtful, he did not pursue a writing career. After saying "wow" to what I thought was just stating the obvious, he thanked me for the compliment but went on to say that he could have just assumed that I looked down on folks like him for not being as "brave."

He had used that word once before when I admitted via text that I bet my mom wished I had pursued something more stable, as he had. "You were different," he said in response. "You were braver."

I wish I had the confidence of others who actually aren't shit but get booed up anyway. Brother, can you spare a cup of misplaced confidence? I wish I had been honest sooner. Maybe things might have gone differently. Or perhaps not—but if nothing else, I would have made my best effort.

While walking with him back home, he asked how I felt about my life changing. I expressed to him that it's not changing as sharply as some believe it to be, but I do feel as if I am working toward getting over certain humps. He asked me how important money was to my future. My answer was immediate: "It's everything. I am not trying to struggle anymore."

He countered the way a thoughtful, socially conscious person who quit a job for one that felt like it mattered more in terms of contributions to society is expected to: stressing that money wasn't the end all, be all. Or the key to happiness.

Yeah, yeah, I get that lesson, but in terms of my life, having financial security means I can embark on the kind of freedom I've long been deprived of. The kind of life he was living. You have to be able to afford choice. Happiness is expensive. I have made conscious choices about the direction of my life and how I wanted it to go, but money plays a direct influence in whether much of those plans come to fruition. He's right to a larger extent. But I'll take the money for now.

MAMA'S BOY

I worry that ultimately, this experience has been just another way of me disappointing you. You are correct in that I care too much about what you think. I am a grown man. I do not need to be so consumed with what my mother thinks of me, an adult male. Maybe he was right that Marcus and I are both mama's boys. He was right about a few other things, too, to his brown liquor-scented credit.

You can be mean. Not just cold, which was always more attributable to those who were cruel to you rather than any testament to your character. You are a kind, compassionate person regardless of whatever outward disposition you decide to deliver at the time. But yes, you can be mean and are efficient in using that ability to make people feel small. I don't fault you for that, actually. People made you mean. You can indeed be a little holier than thou. He isn't the only one to think that, though he always deserved your scorn.

You were not abusive, but you, like a lot of Black parents of a certain time, gave in to corporal punishment at times. The practice should die altogether because no matter the intention, when you strike your child, you are hitting them with your force, and what informs that force isn't always purely rooted in some effort to discipline. Can you imagine a child getting a whopping from a Black parent living in Trump's America? No ass should be swatted extra hard because of that man's policies or his infuriating tweets. You had a lot of stress in and out of your home. I could see that stress leading to a mis-aim here and there. But you never whopped *me*.

The worst you've ever made me feel in terms of disciplining me was the time you made me stand in the corner for what felt like forever as you finished watching *The Young and the Restless*. I assume you knew the best way to punish each kid, but did you ever get the sense if you struck me so harshly that I would hit you back? I never wanted to do that, but Dad wasn't the only parent who could get it. You were mostly on the defensive, but there were times he pushed you to take the first swing. Still, I saw the way you struck in other situations.

You did not hit me that way. Then again, none of us were ever much trouble, and I was relatively quiet by comparison. I was never really as sneaky as I was portrayed to be in that house. It was a punch line that became my reputation solely based on repetition. Even if I were sneaky, we were conditioned to be secretive. It would simply make me a product of my environment, ma'am.

But when I did cause trouble—fights, suspensions, in-school suspensions, being kicked out of class at times because like you, when I feel pushed to my limit, I lash out verbally (to start)—you didn't hit me then either. You must have known the resentment I had wasn't limited to him. You must have seen it in my eyes. Like you, I don't have a game face. People always know what we are thinking. We say we'll try to change that, but we're both saying it to be saying it. We don't especially care. We kind of both revel in it, no?

I've been back home for a spell or two, but for the most part, I haven't really behaved like a person who truly lives and exists in Houston in so long. So you must have seen the contempt I had for you both at one point scratched into the walls by now. How did it make you feel? Probably not as amused as when you saw "Batman" scratched into the walls in me and Marcus's closet. Remember when I kept telling you that I wanted to be Batman? You found it so amusing. I still want to be Batman. I wish I knew someone.

I have never had the nerve to say it in person, but I am very sorry for what I wrote into the walls. Whenever I do come home for the holidays, I often stay with you and you make up my old bed. You had to have come across "DIE MOM AND DAD" scratched into the walls. I have written about what I felt when I wrote it, but I should have long considered the impact of that on others. You might have seen it every single time you reached to the other side of the bed as you tucked in the fitted sheet, evened out the flat sheet you laid down after, and topped them with the comforter.

I am really sorry, Mama. I was in pain, but it was reactionary. Disgustingly impulsive. Where do I get that from? Him, huh? I love him, but I don't want to be like him—surely not in those ways. I regret the day I grabbed that butter knife and soiled that wall you purchased with your hard-earned money by turning it into my journal entry. I shared that in writing, but not with the apology the act commanded.

Of course, I would have never wanted to strike you, my

mother. I was angry, though. You kept me in that angry house and wouldn't let me go out and be social. You were apparently worried about the outside forces influencing me, yet everything I witnessed in that house is responsible for the overwhelming majority of my character flaws, past and present. I wouldn't have wanted to touch you in any way that didn't emphatically convey love and adoration, but I would have never stood there and let you strike me. Nothing—my height, my weight, my age, your authority—would have stopped me from fighting back. Because my thought was always *You have your fucking nerve.*

All of the shit we were enduring plus your restrictions and you wanted to take out your rage on me? No, no, no. You don't get that. Not without a fight anyway. I would have not had it. I would have gone down fighting. It's what I always thought when I saw you pop off. I meant it with every thing in me.

This is not to say any child in the house was Penny Gordon from *Good Times.* You were not an abuser and we were not abused—at least not by your hands. But you know, Black folks sure can discipline hard. In ways we ought to frown upon now. And that is not to say I was miraculously braver. Your daughter is the strongest of us all. We were all a little scared of you.

But my original point still stands: You treated me a little bit differently, and I've always wondered if it was because you could smell the whiff of defiance in me.

My anger mainly drove that defiance. We all joke about how short you are, but you're the David of Lafayette and ready to chomp down Goliaths from all over. I had a rage in me that wanted to bring that entire house down. It blossomed in that setting. Those feelings were nourished more than any others in my formative years.

I suspect you knew that.

We've only talked about it once as adults. You, in your sixties, proclaiming to be far less concerned with how the words that came out of your mouth sounded when everyone who loves you knows you never cared that much to begin with. Me, in my thirties, still longing for us to have been more open with our feelings in the past—knowing most efforts to have these conversations have ended in failure, but nevertheless, the sissy persisted.

This time, it went well. I was pleasantly surprised. I wanted to make a note of it at the time, but you would have swatted my sentimental ass away and turned the volume up on your gospel tunes. But I think we were both ready to address it.

That quiet anger we both possess.

When Dad loses his shit, he wants it to command everyone's attention. A lot of people are like this. They want you to know when they are mad and act as if it requires a town crier. They don't have time to dilly-dally waiting for one, so they take on the role themselves. He is a little Fry Daddy that way.

We simmer, on the other hand. And stew. We are so used to things being awful, but while we may vocalize our displeasure, we're not necessarily mad. It takes a lot for us to get mad-mad. A lot of it has to do with our fear that once we allow ourselves to get angry, it becomes uncontrollable. It's a force that takes over because no matter what in the present prompted our fury, it comes with a lifetime of residual anger. It's hard to contain that lividity once it's out there.

I gave Chris a black eye on the bus because he called you gay. He wouldn't leave me alone. He kept taunting how gay I acted. How gay I sounded. Then he called you gay and that's when everything turned black. All I can remember is shouting "Who's a bitch now?" as the bus driver who I bet wasn't paid enough to be dealing with this pulled me off of him. That wasn't the first time it happened.

It happened with Jarick in third grade. And Gilberto in fourth grade. And Gregory in sixth. I didn't start any of these fights, but even if I finished them there was always a caveat: Each fight took place around the time Dad got out of order. But he was so frequent in his fury that no matter how sweet I was and tried to be, the anger was there.

However, I really didn't want to fight Ebony in ninth grade. She wanted notebook paper, and while I was normally generous, I barely had any left and needed it to last for the rest of the week. But she snatched it out of my hands and stormed away with it. So I got up and went after my paper. Then she punched me. Like a nigga.

We were friendly since middle school, and here she was, punching me over some fucking notebook paper. It was college ruled, not that it matters. I could not believe she did that. What in the hood bitch hell?

I was still chubby and short then. She was taller and bigger than I was. She looked like a fake-ass Lady of Rage. And she claimed to have sold something called cheese. She showed it to me once. It wasn't really yellow; I guess I could say it was tan. I didn't learn until much later that cheese was black tar heroin mixed with crushed Tylenol PM tablets. Motherfuckers are inventive. Turns out, middle school students and high school students use it. She put it in my hand. I was not impressed. I dropped that right back to her. I didn't want to run the risk of those drug-sniffing dogs that we used to see from time to time at Madison getting a whiff and biting my hand off or something. Let her deal with Officer Cujo.

When she punched me, I took it. I stood there. I was not

going to hit her back. Normally, if you hit me, I am swinging and best of luck to you. But not her. That was a girl. I was not going to do that. I told myself I would never, ever, ever, ever hit a woman. I would not be like him. I would never do that. I could not do that. To do that would destroy me.

That's why I stood there. She taunted me for it. She laughed. Called me a lot of names. Some of the names Dad would call you. I didn't want any problems; I just wanted my paper back.

Then she pushed me. Hard. The class was watching. It was a classroom run by someone who didn't have the range to demand respect and wrestle control back from the students who obviously intimidated him. Catering to that audience, she swung again. I ducked, I grabbed her by her weave ponytail, and we fought.

She was a big motherfucker so she kept swinging, but it was too late. She unleashed me. I only remember grabbing her by the hair, bringing her down to my height, and letting my anger—no longer quiet, not yearning to remain dormant—take over. We knocked over desks, or maybe, I knocked over desks. We fell to the ground. I had to be pulled off of her.

I was sent to the class next door. I had to go see the vice principal. I forgot his name, but that lanky Black with the curl that looked crafted by a box is who they sent me to. But first, one of my classmates got me. Since she was another girl, I just knew she was going to be mad at me.

"You beat that bitch ass!" is what she shouted gleefully as she tried to dab me up. No, sis. We're not there yet. Ebony's nose was bloody and her weave ponytail was in her hand. We walked together with Vice Principal Silky Hair From A Box to the office.

I was so worried about what you were going to say when I

got home. I was so embarrassed to see you and my sister. I was prepared to be rightfully put down. I might have actually lain down had you struck me in that moment.

You weren't mad at me. As you explained to me then, you were told what happened and how extremely hard I had tried to not get into a fight with a girl, but the girl was determined to have a fight with me. And my three-day suspension was scaled back to one after my Pre-AP English teacher found out what happened. He talked about what a good student I was, and because he, too, heard about how it went down, he felt an equitable punishment was unfair in this circumstance.

Ebony ended up apologizing and acted like nothing ever happened. Yeah, this was some hood shit. All's well did not end well. I could not get over what happened. You not being mad at me was not enough.

I have not been in a fight ever since.

I resisted the temptation the few other times I felt provocation coming at high school. It was to be expected; the nickname for the place was "Madhouse." I learned to settle myself. In the past, while I might not have swung first, I knew how to trap someone into giving me a reason to swing back at them. I had decided that no matter how mad I got, it was better not to put myself in that situation unless the situation once again forced itself on me.

I almost did get in another fight some years later at the club. I'll never know what that dude's problem was. He kept bumping me. He said he'd beat my ass. I would have let it go had he not bucked to me one too many times. Marcus stopped that fight from happening. He said I would not be fighting in the club and potentially catching any cases while in college. It's a good thing he separated us. I am quick and I saw a bottle I could have cracked his face open with. He could have caught that to his face with a force fueled by some twenty-plus years of pent-up angst and frustration.

However, I wouldn't say I lost my cool in that instance. That was some ho ass bitch with a chip on his shoulder. I was merely prepared to let it be what it was if he decided to take that swing. After Marcus broke us up, we went back to dancing. We used to go off together to Hurricane Chris's "A Bay Bay." You have always been so tickled by that song. It took you back to growing up in Louisiana. You were related to someone they called "Bay Bay." I loved how amused you were whenever it played on the radio.

My anger would rise like the humidity in Houston in summer, but trust me, I learned how to cool down. If I didn't get ahold of myself and my emotions, I knew who I would turn out like.

The only other time I lost my cool was the first year I moved to New York. It was a few months after my thirtieth birthday, which you hadn't acknowledged until I called you right before I celebrated with those who cared more about the day than you did that year. You usually call at my exact time of birth—3:24 p.m. CST, or somewhere in that vicinity—every year to confirm when it is exactly my birthday. But you were upset with me. I reminded you that I was gay and talking about it.

We didn't talk much for months. You wouldn't have wanted to hear about much of what I had going on at the time. I had started dating someone. A man. I know. Who had a man. I know, I know.

I looked myself in the mirror and quoted Monica's "Sideline Ho," the best song from the painfully underrated album *The Makings of Me*: "You's a ho. You's a ho. Sideline ho." I also sang a little bit of MoKenStef's "He's Mine" while cruising through both his and his boyfriend's Facebook pages. I began to make peace with my reality.

As it turns out, he was dating me, his boyfriend, and somebody else he met the same day he met me. Realizing how unfair he was being to all of us (despite my being a willing participant), he eventually made a decision: not me or the boyfriend. I didn't take this well. For the first week I tried to be rational and said all of the things that you tell yourself when shit blows up in your face: *You knew what it was when you got involved.* Blah, blah, ha ha, you sideline ho, etc.

I ended up at that same bar I met him at with a friend who, at the time, didn't appreciate the value of "woosah." I ended up carrying her out of the club. She wanted to throw a drink in the face of the dude in defense of me, which I did not ask for or approve of.

We got into a cab and left. I told her I was fine. But I really wasn't. I broke into tears. Crying makes me uncomfortable, so I washed it away with anger and unleashed a fury on Sixth Avenue that had me kicking over people's bikes, various trash cans, and pushing over newsstands. Apparently I made my way back to the bar to yell a lot of not nice things about him. Another friend, Alex, had to come down to restrain me and remind me about the consequences of a Black man acting like a damn fool in the West Village.

"You can't be kicking down white people's bikes."

He was so right. Never give them a reason to turn you into a hashtag, and you, another grieving Black mother.

Although I knew it was over—he made a choice and it wasn't me, plus I now looked crazy as shit—I apologized days later. Repeatedly. He accepted. We talked for some weeks after the incident, but I had to let him go. The last thing he told me was that I smelled good. I left it at that and considered it closure. Then I ended up seeing him once a year later and then it was the kind of closure that lives up to the definition.

That's the last time I can recall allowing my anger to get the best of me in such extremity. The ordeal exposed that I was better, but needed to work a lot harder to control my anger. To not let someone else allow me to get that upset. To not allow myself to get that pissed off, no matter the perceived provocation.

I made a real effort to control that quiet anger.

We were talking about quiet anger in the setting we do most of our convos of depth: your car, riding home from the airport. I didn't say all of this to you. I knew my audience. Still, I said enough to paint a picture of someone carrying baggage who doesn't want to let it take me whole or take down some innocent bystander.

It felt good to hear you say you have struggled with that same degree of quiet anger. The kind not everyone can spot, but if you suffer from it, too, you can at least sense it in another. It doesn't carry a stench, but we can sniff each other out.

Since I was eighteen years old, you are the only person to have picked me up from the airport and dropped me off. You have rearranged your work schedule in order to keep that going. Was it because you wanted to make sure you saw me for the last time should the unthinkable happen? We never really discussed that, but that's how I have always taken it. I have loved that so much about you. It's the unspoken tenderness to you. It's one of the things about you that makes me love you so much, Mama.

It's only been one time since you didn't pick me up and

drop me off at the airport. When I came home for a book event in Houston. For my very first book. I know grudges aren't in vogue (by the way, I wish the original former members of the R&B group En Vogue would reunite and make some of that Xscape and SWV tour money—they can keep the new member from *The Jamie Foxx Show* if they must), but I still cannot believe that major bookstore rejected my publisher's request to do an event there only to randomly tell my brother when he went out to buy a copy of the book that I should do something there. But shout-out to Brazos Books, an indie bookstore, for a superb event with a room full of old high school classmates, family members, and the lovely white people and other non-Blacks who heard me talking to Terry Gross when I blessedly appeared on *Fresh Air*.

You don't know about any of this because you wanted no part of it. You never did approve of me "telling my business." You always told me that information can be weaponized. Your other concern was that "those people"—who I interpreted as white folks—were allowing me to ride the wave of something that society is pretending okay but isn't—the gay shit—and they would eventually let me falter. But, as you always added, you would be there for me when that happened. It is a delightfully passive-aggressive pledge, but you mean it.

I never blamed you for not trusting white folks as a collective. You helped integrate a high school and were attacked for it. You are a Black woman and daughter of the South. You have every reason to be suspicious no matter your age, but because you were born in the 1950s, you know how ripe their contempt for us can be. You have seen so many be propped up only to be taken down. You were protective for good reason.

But I've always known you to judge people individually. You

were fine with white people and all types of people in that regard. As a nurse and as a Christian (not perfect, but no one is, and my criticisms notwithstanding, you're one of the best ones I know), your capacity for compassion and decency was extended to all. It's why that Saudi Royal wanted to hire you and whisk you and yours away to his home country to take care of his wife and family. Not that you would have ever done that. You are a traditionalist culturally, but you are the type to literally swing at any form of a woman's subjugation. And again, you're Catholic and you mean that shit, ma'am. That's why you didn't go away with him or any of those other very rich foreigners who tried to woo you away.

You've never said it, but I get the feeling some of these people just wanted you for non-medical reasons. You've never owned how beautiful you are. You were discouraged from believing it because your complexion wasn't fair enough and your hair was not as straight as someone hoped for it to be. You are stunning, though. I've seen your old pictures. I see your face as I write these words. You are so pretty and I'm not only saying that because I see you whenever I look in the mirror at my own face.

We are twins in some ways and maybe that's always been the underlying problem.

When you didn't pick me up, it stung, but it was for the best. I went over to see you anyway. To say I loved you even as I listened to you vocalize your disapproval. Mainly because you know and I know that you'll either get over it or I'll continue in spite of it. With your support, no less. You are always rooting for me even if you aren't for what it is I have to say and share.

I think you always sensed that creative spirit in me. Marcus's surfaced early, too, but I reckon—yeah, reckon, and I bet you can hear me exactly how I sound it . . . I'm so goofy—you knew how determined I was. That I was trying to figure out how I could be like those people on television.

Remember when I asked you about my cousin that was a CNN anchor? I saw the name Arceneaux and felt something different that morning. I always thought the last name Arceneaux was cool even if other people couldn't spell it or pronounce it. I felt a sense of pride seeing that name on a chyron.

I never connected with her, though, outside of a brief call nearly a decade after I saw her on TV. I was a freshman in college then, majoring in broadcast journalism. She was polite, but the conversation was brief and we never spoke again. I had heard she had some health issues later, but I never begrudged her in any way. She knew my father, not me. I didn't know any of those people—the Arceneauxs—really. I may never know them. But that was just an aside. I'm used to not knowing them. I was more interested in meeting people who could help me achieve my dreams. I did my best to make the most out of this overpriced, debt-riddled excursion into higher education and the access it provided. I am so grateful to you and your credit score. I am so sorry it's taken longer than anticipated to pay you back.

As many times as I have fallen, you have refused to let me stay down. You are too tough for that. And you know I am not weak, and thus needn't behave as such. You may not quite understand what I do for a living. Hell, I don't. I'm learning as I go.

But you do know that I have struggled and there is a guilt I have carried for feeling like a bad return on your investment. Publicity is not money and there are people who find less value in me over the identity you felt best to shield for different reasons. Or maybe that was part of your calculation. You don't know media and television, but you know white people and you know America.

I remember big sis once saying, "I'm sorry you weren't born to a rich white family." I don't remember the context, but while I don't make apologies for dreaming big, I am sorry for not factoring in how difficult and how expensive it was going to be to put myself in the position to pursue many of the opportunities that come much easier to white people. All of the people whose careers I admired were white men. It wasn't their whiteness I was attracted to; I didn't and don't want to be white. It was the type of work they did that I gravitated toward. It appealed to me. I knew I could do the same quality of work, only in my way. I only wanted to show I was no less capable and no less deserving. I knew it wouldn't be easy, but I can admit that perhaps I didn't know how many attempts would be made to humble me.

I'm sorry I didn't take that into greater account.

We never talk about any of this at great length. My work has always been a touchy subject. Not only is it too personal now, the benefits still haven't outweighed the debt I took on to get there. None of it has yet to significantly scale back the balance on all those loans. The ones your names are attached to.

That, probably more than anything, is what I am sorry about.

You do not want me to be sorry. It's done. There is no going back. You've said this so many times to me. You had your concerns, but you did this for me. I worry guilt factored into that decision a little bit.

As much as I complain about the debt, what eats me about it is that while I did have lofty dreams, it took me into my thirties to acknowledge that careerist purists alone were not why I fled. I needed to get out of that house and be far from the city no matter how I loved it because it all felt suffocating. I could never be at peace there because no one around seemed to want to help me put some of the parts broken in me back together. But we're all a bit broken, as lovely folks as we all are.

I, too, have wondered if you sensed that. You are so perceptive. You are such a good observer. I get that from you. I can talk and talk and talk, but I know how to be silent and observe my surroundings just as well. You lent me a life raft and your reward was being chained to my debt.

Had we known better, we could have gone about all of this differently, but as you said, it's done. I still want to say I'm sorry. I'm going to be sorry until the last payment is made—maybe even after that. I want you to forgive me, even if you don't think I need to be forgiven. You have not allowed me to feel like a self-centered bastard. You meant your apology well over a decade ago. Why can't I accept it?

The fear lingers—specifically the one where I question if I grew up to become another man who let you down. That is something I alone have to make peace with. I will try harder.

I am proud of the work I have done, even if I have never explicitly said it to you. It is work that has been undervalued, and while money may not be everything, we live in a capitalist society. Our value is collectively judged by the metric of how much we have to show for it. I don't have enough yet to show. I want to be bigger than such superficial influencing, but it's been drilled into my psyche so the shrinkage seeps in sometimes.

I can go without your approval on who I love and who I want to have sex with. I can live with your horror that I could end up in hell. What I cannot stomach is to leave this world in a state worse than the one I entered through my parents. That's already happened to so many through no real fault of their own. People fall under a system designed for their perpetual stumble.

Nevertheless, I don't want to become one of them.

What good is any of this if that's how it ends?

I don't think that is my fate, but to have carried some of the burdens of my twenties into my thirties has shaken my faith. You have long worried about my faith levels. I have a strong spirit, but it has been beaten down. I still have a lot of fight in me, but I am tired. You can hear it in my voice. It's with you when the confidence I try to exude with everyone else instantly melts at the sound of your voice.

I'm still fighting, though, Mama. God is with me. I'm just not at church. I can already hear you: "Mmhmm, go to God's house." I'll go with you to Christmas mass again. You know you were happy that I invited myself the last time.

You wait for your reward in the afterlife. I still want you to have paradise now. I want to be able to give that to you. There is no one on Earth that I think deserves it more. You do not care for monetary things and never will, but I will find a way to repay the debt I owe you. I am determined.

If anything, even when I get over the hump—truly and finally—you will continue to disapprove of my methodology. You will not approve of this lingering defiance to break mores and tell my business. The irony then, now, and forever more will be that nothing I do in this world will have happened without you. You may find your religious objections to be in accord with the divine, but what makes me see God in you is you finding it in your heart to not only love me through disagreement and disappointment, but to make evident that no matter what, you will be there.

That has meant more than any rosary you have ever sent me. Or novenas in the mail to make sure I am praying. Or even the cookies and pralines you baked and sent me, though they for sure have been the most satisfying.

Love is complicated. We both know that for varied reasons. But when it is true, it is pure, and there is none purer than a mother's love for her child. You have proven that more times than I could ever count. Again, I am going to find a way to pay you back.

Until then, I'm still so sorry even though you don't want me to be.

TO FREEDOM

In the midst of writing this book, one that is largely themed around the varied ways in which student loan debt can consume one's life and impair so many different facets of it, a billionaire and two actual populists all introduced a different possibility for those marred by student loan debt. One was an act of benevolence (or bluster, depending on who you are asking), the other part of a more ambitious idea to reimagine higher education in America. Both represented a type of freedom that I have long yearned for but have yet to attain.

On what was described by many as a muggy Sunday morning in Atlanta, Robert F. Smith, a billionaire investor and philanthropist, stood before 396 graduating students at Morehouse College ready to change the trajectory of their lives. Initially, his commencement address sounded typical. He talked about the remarkable life that got him an invitation to speak in front of these fancy Black folks in the first place. For Smith, part of that story began at Carson Elementary, a very well-to-do school with a predominately well-to-do white population far, far away from the part of Denver where he resided. He declared he'd never forget having to take the No. 13 bus to get to Carson.

"Those five years drastically changed the trajectory of my life," he explained. "The teachers at Carson were extraordinary. They embraced me and challenged me to think critically and start to move toward my full potential. I, in turn, came to real- ize at a young age that the white kids and the Black kids, the Jewish kids and the one Asian kid were all pretty much the same."

Doesn't this sound like the ending of some sanitized biopic released from a major Hollywood studio? Doesn't matter which one. They're all put through the same rinse. Forgive me, *Sesame Street* taught me better than this. At our core, we all indeed are pretty much the same, but I did look for Barney and Baby Bop for a second as I watched Smith deliver his remarks. I believe Smith's story to be true, but on its surface, the beginning re- marks suggested this would be a solid tale but not the kind to rile up a bunch of Black folks sweating profusely because it's May in Atlanta, Georgia, and they're sitting outside, shaking and baking.

It was when Smith deviated from his prepared remarks— which were nice if you read them in full—his commencement address became one that will live in infamy.

"My family is going to create a grant to eliminate your student loans!" he announced.

It was a stark contrast to comments former President Obama made in his Morehouse commencement address in 2013.

"We know that too many young men in our community continue to make bad choices," he said. "Growing up, I made a few myself. And I have to confess, sometimes I wrote off my own failings as just another example of the world trying to keep a Black man down. But one of the things you've learned over the last four years is that there's no longer any room for excuses. I understand that there's a common fraternity creed here at Morehouse: 'Excuses are tools of the incompetent, used to build bridges to nowhere and monuments of nothingness.'"

The lecturing, infuriating as it was, continued.

"We've got no time for excuses—not because the bitter legacies of slavery and segregation have vanished entirely; they haven't. Not because racism and discrimination no longer exist; that's still out there. It's just that in today's hyper-connected, hyper-competitive world, with a billion young people from China and India and Brazil entering the global workforce alongside you, nobody is going to give you anything you haven't earned. And whatever hardships you may experience because of your race, they pale in comparison to the hardships previous generations endured—and overcame."

I will never forget seeing then presidential candidate Barack Obama at the Toyota Center inspiring me in ways I never found previously conceivable as a child born under Reagan and raised under Bush I, Clinton, and Bush II, a time that included recession, economic booms that didn't hit my family the same way, and mass incarceration that resulted in many of the other Black boys I grew up around finding themselves in and out of jail. I could have never imagined a Black president and then it became the standard.

Still, for all the reasons I liked him—his gifts as a writer and orator, his intellect, his wife, his children, his sarcastic wit, and his ability to dance poorly but not look too embarrassing—there were parts of President Obama that irked the hell out of me: most of them rooted in how he would scold Black people on the virtues of individual responsibility while not speaking as boldly on the conditions we are subjected to that place us at a significant disadvantage.

There's much to celebrate about his administration—I have written as much in my work—but consider the period where he delivered these remarks. In that period, he was criticized for the timidity in which he tackled the foreclosure crisis, which devastated Black America, and housing segregation, which continues to hurt Black people most. The students he was speaking to were plausibly already affected by the former and would be impacted by the latter in their futures.

When some made this distinction between Obama's remarks and Smith's at the time, many Black folks took off and metaphorically lathered their face in Vaseline, ready to scrap on behalf of the first Black president. But he only looked Messianic on that one *Rolling Stone* cover during the 2008 Democratic presidential primary. He ain't never been Jesus for real.

It wasn't about whether or not Obama should have paid off the debt of the 2013 graduating class of Morehouse College; it was about understanding that this country presents unique challenges to Black people, and no matter how much those challenges shift with time, they speak to systematic barriers all the same. So if you are not giving your all in the pursuit of dismantling those barriers, you don't have the right to stand before a group of Black men at a historically Black college and tell them racism isn't that big of a deal anymore, so suck it up. Sadly, we don't all find our way to care from a nice, well-off-enough white family who can put us in the best of schools that provide us the type of access that can help eliminate whatever debts were taken on along the journey at a faster rate than the typical Black American's.

Robert Smith at least made a real gesture, and for that, national hero was born in the news. Well, to many of us, anyway. For many, Robert Smith doing a nice thing is actually a terrible thing. To others, being generous to some is wrong because it teaches the wrong lesson.

In "Grand gesture: Morehouse donor teaches grads the wrong lesson," from the Editorial Board of the *Pittsburgh Post-Gazette*, they write: "There's something to be said for paying what you owe, for holding up your end of a bargain."

As they see it: "It is unfortunate that many colleges are high-priced; that students don't really understand the magnitude of the encumbrance they're undertaking when they choose higher education that is beyond their reasonable means; and that their parents don't guide them toward more affordable options like community college, state universities or technical schools."

I can understand questions related to how exactly such a grand gesture made by Smith can be actually executed, but this editorial board's gripe is about the donation itself. Smith's intentions were to make life easier for 396 college students who already had enough going against them for simply being Black men living in America. Those disadvantages are magnified by socioeconomic factors that can be directly traced to institutional barriers. Say, the very debt he offered to handle on their behalf. The editorial board sees this as a freebie given away to folks not holding up their "end of a bargain." What this editorial board—more than likely filled with white men and women, like many newsrooms across the country—fail to realize is that Black folks aren't offered a fair bargain to begin with.

What type of people feign such allegiance to a bargain rooted in bias? The kind of folks who if they don't directly benefit from said bias already, aspire to. After all, this is the same paper that did not technically endorse a 2016 presidential candidate, but was slammed for offering a "pseudo endorsement" of Sweet Potato Saddam at the time. As you read the editorial board's "A guide to decide: Twelve tests to choose between Clinton and Trump," where their allegiances lean are thinly veiled but very much identifiable. In their test for "economic growth," the nod is given to Donald Trump "not only because he is new, and not just because he has committed to tax cuts for small business, for estates, and for the middle class, but because he is a businessman and a total pragmatist."

Donald Trump is a stupid-ass bitch who, thanks to a *New York Times* investigation, was found to have received the equivalent today of at least $413 million from his father's real estate empire. Then there are the tales of how alleged creative accounting helped him not just shave off tax liabilities but actually enrich himself by blowing through his daddy's money.

I tried to hold back the vomit rising in my mouth as I read on, but true to form, the lies worsened: "He understands money, he understands power, and he is impatient with inaction." And: "He is dynamic—a builder and deal maker. Being the ultimate political outsider, Mr. Trump, again, has the freedom to experiment. And we need something of the New Deal spirit now—willingness to try new things and throw out what has clearly failed."

Donald Trump shares Franklin D. Roosevelt's fancy for internment camps and habit of trafficking in racism, but the New Deal spirit? That piece reads as erotica for the demented, but notice how favorable the treatment is for the proven failure whose entire narrative can be attributed to privilege and pillage compared to that for these Black men being given only a small fraction of the kind of leg up the sons of rich white men get.

If any of us default on our student loans, our lives are ruined. We are condemned for not holding up our end of the bargain. We are considered to be examples of failure. Our credit will be destroyed, and in turn, it impairs our ability to work, to gain housing, and to effectively function the way a "responsible adult" is expected to.

Sweet Potato Saddam doesn't pay any of his loans back and is rewarded with more loans, and miraculously, further mythologized as an example of "the freedom to experiment." If Donald Trump were Black, they would find every which way to describe him as a shiftless, bottom-feeding nigger who needs to start taking some personal responsibility for his irresponsibility. At best, he would have been Flavor Flav's coworker on *The Surreal Life*, not the star of *The Apprentice*.

If he were a woman, the *Pittsburgh Post-Gazette* wouldn't have found his long list of failures so aspirational either.

The *Pittsburgh Post-Gazette* is but one paper espousing the mindset that people—especially Black people—are getting perceived free handouts. It's a mindset typical of how conservatives respond to the topic of implicit bias, the racism that informs it, and the ways in which we tackle it.

As for New Deal Don, by the end of 2017, Trump along with Republicans in Congress had passed a $1.5 trillion tax bill. I'm more of a Joy-Ann Reid and Chris Hayes viewer than I am a Jim Cramer or Kelly Evans one, but I've watched *Billions* and somehow passed economics in college, so let me try to explain this in a way that won't even give me a headache. The crux of the bill goes as follows: Corporations pay less than they already do, as do the other very, very rich people. As for anyone else, despite initial touting that it was a "middle class tax bill" from that apricot-hued asshole and budding tyrant, that was hardly the case. In other words, it was some wealthy white folks doing a money grab. Think Joanne the Scammer if Joanne had the backing of a major political party whose power was rooted in being financially backed by the wealthiest people in our society, along with the exploitation of our electorate's prejudices and certain governmental systems that were designed with their racism in mind. For example, the electoral college that helped pave the way for all of this.

As fate would have it, a little over a month after Smith made his charitable pledge that rubbed some right-leaning know-it-alls with a paternalistic streak the wrong way, it was revealed that the GOP-led tax bill was the bust opponents for non-plutocrats bill predicted it would be.

The nonpartisan Congressional Research Service followed the U.S. economy's performance in the first full year following the legislation going into law and found that lowering corporate tax rates from 35 percent to 21 percent not only led to a 31 percent drop in corporate tax revenue (almost two times steeper than originally forecasted by economists), but did not generate any meaningful new economic growth. Even better, data has shown that those who made less than $25,000 had a higher chance of being audited last year than those making between $200,000 and $500,000. So the bill many argued would only reinforce structural inequities has done exactly that. Around the time I graduated from college, similar GOP-crafted policy led to the greatest economic catastrophe since the Great Depression, and that gave way to a bailout. A smooth decade later, the ultra-rich were getting yet another giveaway.

I'm no Suze Orman, but it sounds like folks like her need to quit pretending so many of us are financially screwed because of our new, unearned love of oak milk lattes and look elsewhere to explain the widening gap. I sure shouldn't be upset with Robert Smith, who has a personal invitation to become my new benefactor and bestie. Granted, it is not lost on me that these very tax laws have helped Smith maintain the sizable wealth that allows him to be so giving.

It was a point the *New York Times* editorial board made in their own editorial "We Are Applauding the 'Gift' of an Affordable Education. Something Has Gone Wrong."

In it, they lament: "A new generation of plutocrats has amassed great fortunes, in part because the federal government has minimized the burden of taxation. Americans once again are reduced to applauding acts of philanthropy necessitated by failures of policy."

From their vantage point, "Closing that loophole would be a much better graduation present for the class of 2019." I understand and share the underlying frustrations expressed. As a Black person of a working class family who did not have access to any of the benefits others enjoy and often blames myself for taking out these loans just trying to have even a smidgen of what others got, I, too, am angry over how flawed this system is. But as a Black person struggling with debt because I went to a school like Morehouse College—in my case, Howard University—no matter the politics and bad policies behind it, it was nice to see a Black man come to the aid of other Black men.

In addition to these editorials floating around, I noticed some across social media also took umbrage with Smith's donation. Some have elected to interpret these acts not as ones of mercy or bold but necessary moves needed in order to right an egregious wrong that has led to more than a trillion dollars in debt that threatens the greater economy; instead, they signify something else: a handout. How utterly boring. Such is an attitude steeping in selfishness and soiled by delusion—namely this idea that we live in a meritocracy. To them, if they have managed to either pay off their debts or never taken any on to begin with, why can't the rest of us do the same?

It's a question that sounds simple only to the simple-minded.

That degree of selfish thinking took me back to my *New York Times* essay about my plight with private student loan debt that started this journey to talk about it publicly, and the less than compassionate responses it generated from a few like-minded fuck-offs.

I try not to read the comments, but when prodded by a friend to give a look, I did and was quickly reminded why I never read the comments. One in particular stood out. I won't give her name, but she's a white woman who lives in the Midwest. She's probably the wife of one of those white blue collar workers the political press swears matter more than everyone else at the polls.

She started off her remarks by sharing, "I always have a problem with sob stories such as this." She asked why I chose Howard University and not Rice University. She mentioned grants. I can tell she does not know how much Rice University costs. Not to mention, when I consider many of the opportunities I have enjoyed in the midst of my struggles, most of them were directly related to being able to attend Howard University.

Nevertheless, she carried on.

She told me that my choice to be a writer and knowing that I had to pay an obscene amount of money a month in student loan repayments was "another bad choice." Career advice followed: "Why not have taken a job with a good salary and made a big head start on those loans, and used weekend spare time to start writing, writing when the loan was smaller?" I wish I could get a job tutoring her on reading comprehension because I pretty much explained a lot of that in the original essay. I make a lot more than the median U.S. income, but the structure of my debt—which my lender refuses to bend on—is what put me in the predicament I was speaking to. That along with so many outside factors simply beyond my control.

If I had any doubt from the tone in which her commentary began, this is when I knew she was white: "My father was the youngest of 10 children, and was born in 1901. College was the exception in his small southern MO town—far from the rule. It took him 7 years to finish college at the Univ of MO. He would go to school for a year, and then teach for a year (possible in those days)."

To hell with her pops. What does his experience have to do with mine? What do you think my Black relatives of that era were facing at the time? There were countless other commenters with thoughts along similar lines, but they're all equally useless to me. I love when white people lecture me on oppression. I love when they pretend we live in a society that if you work hard, you will be rewarded. To be fair, some nonwhites do this, too, and yeah, they can join them in the tarpit with the others who speak on circumstances they know nothing about. Most of us who deal with this debt will concede our mistake, but that does not negate how in many ways, we were pushed to that decision.

Still, that lack of empathy and refusal for mercy is why not everyone could fully embrace what remains something to be celebrated. Smith's act of generosity came at a time when the U.S. government is stepping up its efforts to collect on student loan debt even as it does nothing to combat its origins (and how those factors hurt Black college students and graduates the most).

Smith's gesture was momentous, but it was a move others were making, though with far less capital to work with. Only a few months before Smith's grand gift, churches like Alfred Street Baptist Church in Alexandria, Virginia, also made headlines for paying off the student loan debt of select parishioners. As I later learned from talking to folks who, unlike my heathen ass, still regularly attend church, that's become a bit of thing depending on how much tithing is collected.

I'm not jealous of Jesus's generosity; you are.

Though I was new to the story of churchgoers pitching in, I was familiar with the general notion of people turning to the charity of others to deal with their loans. Over time, I've seen many folks try to pay off their debt by way of crowdfunding. So have others in media, and rather distastefully, created content around people desperate to not be taken down by Navient or their other preferred oppressive lender of choice.

In 2018, I saw a *Forbes* article entitled "5 Crowdfunding Sites That Will Destroy Your Student Loan Debt." In it, those struggling with student loans who want to virtually shake a cup for money are provided advice on how to best meet their goals. Oh, and what advice it is. You get a doozy of tips such as "come up with a positive, creative name for your campaign" and "consider sending an e-journal to show supporters you're accountable."

Other gems are to basically offer labor in exchange for charity. As in, "you can also offer a reward based on your major, such as artwork from art students or free tax preparation from accounting students." I don't know what the digital equivalent of toilet paper is called, but I would advise every person on

Cardi B's internet to use that article as such. If you're going to instruct people how to beg, at least be good at it. Instead of advising me to launch a GoFundMe entitled "Help Arceneaux Pay Off His Loans So He Won't Have to Sell Ass" with a rewards plan that includes me ghostwriting donors' lengthy emails, memoirs, and iOS press releases for Instagram and Twitter.

That piece reminded me of all of the other stupid student loan debt removal themed ones I've read. The ones that talk about how some twenty-seven-year-old from Oklahoma paid off her six-figure student loan debt by staying at home and eating beans from a dented can bought at the nearest general store for five years straight. There are others creating loan-related content for consumption, but at least they seem, uh, less dense about it.

In 2018, TruTV launched *Paid Off*, a *Family Feud*–like game show where contestants competed for the chance to have their student loans paid off. In the initial promotion of the show, host Michael Torpey noted that he only paid off his student debt after booking a Hanes commercial. At the beginning of each episode, contestants introduce themselves by sharing their debt tales and their major. As for the game itself, they get asked questions such as "What's the most romantic date you can have for under $10?" When a contestant gets eliminated, Torpey sends them to the audience to use the show's red "direct to Congress telephone." On the premiere episode, the first person eliminated used the phone and said, "Hello, Congress, your boy Nico here." No contestant exits without $1,000, but as with any game show, their winnings are taxed.

The call to Congress bit registers as somewhat trivializing, but then again, Congress trivializes far worse the matter of 40 million Americans struggling with more than $1.5 trillion in student loan debt. Kudos all the same to Torpey. While this is a gig for him, he uses it to discuss the issue with the severity it deserves even if his job is tackling it in the context of a game show centered on a crisis.

In an interview with MarketWatch, Torpey said of the problem: "It filters back into some of the equality issues and some of the opportunity issues that are in our country." In his opinion, who is not at fault for our nation's student loan problems are the students and families who are struggling under their debt burdens. "It's bullshit to blame an eighteen-year-old for taking out money to get an education. It's also unfair to look at a family who took out money to support their child's education and say, 'Look, you're stuck now.'"

I wish those who believe otherwise would change their minds, or if nothing else, would light their phones and computers on fire instead of lecturing strangers about why falling victim to an imbalanced system is solely a testament to whatever they supposedly lack personally rather than to the system itself. Of course, none of these things address the crux of the problem. I can cheer the nice rich Black man helping out other Black men because I dream of what freedom from student loan debt looks like and am sincerely thrilled for anyone who can escape the pitfalls I've faced faster and without personal suffering. Yet I know charitable acts made by capitalism's sole deity, the benevolent billionaire, are not broadly replicable. Something more advantageous must be done.

I don't know what will come of 2020 Democratic presidential candidate Elizabeth Warren and her bevy of plans, but one in particular modeled on Smith's act on a systemic scale made me think about what could be.

In her plan, released in April 2019, she called for the wiping away of up to $50,000 in student debt for people with annual incomes of less than $100,000, estimated to be 42 million Americans. For borrowers with higher incomes who find themselves nonetheless keeping their heads above water and making a wave when they can, the debt forgiveness would decline by $1 for every $3 in income over $100,000. Don't ask this child left behind in math to do math, but it sounds like the equivalent of a good Memorial Day sale at Macy's for their student loan debt. Moreover, she called for the government to cover tuition at all two- and four-year public colleges and the expansion of Pell Grants for low-income students by $100 billion. She also pushed for the creation of a $50 billion fund for historically Black colleges and universities.

HBCUs have been especially impacted by the student debt crisis. HBCUs have smaller endowments—no shade, as much as many of us would like to regularly give back to our alma maters, the rent and our debts are so high so we do our best when we can. And the private colleges—like Morehouse College—cost more, which means those students take out bigger loans than their non-private HBCU counterparts. But no matter the school, Black students take on 85 percent more debt than their white counterparts and, by virtue of American racism, find themselves paid less than them after they leave college. This is all happening as Black college graduation rates have hit an all-time high.

Robert Smith might be the Black community's best Bobby since Whitney Houston's ex-husband dropped the *Don't Be Cruel* album, but he alone can't fix this. Nor can crowdsourcing from other debt-ridden Americans. Nor can a game show. Not on the level needed to make a monumental shift in the lives of millions. Only equitable taxation of Smith and others with similar enormous wealth can.

That's how Elizabeth Warren proposes to pay for the $1.25 trillion cost of her plan. She calls it an Ultra-Millionaire Tax, a 2 percent annual tax on 75,000 families with $50 million or more in wealth. "The time for half-measures is over," Warren wrote in her piece on Medium where she unveiled the plan. "My broad cancellation plan is a real solution to our student debt crisis. It helps millions of families and removes a weight that's holding back our economy."

A few months after she revealed the plan as part of her presidential campaign, Warren, still a senator from the state that gave us New Edition, opted to introduce that same plan as a bill with South Carolina congressman James E. Clyburn. "It's time to decide: Are we going to be a country that only helps the rich and powerful get richer and more powerful, or are we going to be a country that invests in its future?" Warren said in a statement.

After that, another Democratic presidential candidate, Bernie Sanders, went further by announcing a proposal that, unlike Warren's, was not subject to income eligibility levels to determine how much relief the average person would receive. Instead, his legislation would cancel $1.6 trillion of student loan undergraduate and graduate debt with no eligibility limitations. It would be paid for with a new tax on Wall Street speculation.

At the press conference where he first introduced the legislation, Sanders said, "This proposal completely eliminates student debt in this country and ends the absurdity of sentencing an entire generation, the millennial generation, to a lifetime of debt for the crime of doing the right thing—and that is going out and getting a higher education."

He went on to add, "The bottom line is we shouldn't be punishing people for getting to higher education. It is time to hit the reset button."

During the 2016 election, some of the most racist emails I received were from Bernie Sanders supporters. Many didn't like my argument that the "Bernie or Bust" position taken during that election was rooted in privilege and only preached as gospel by those more inclined to survive a Trump presidency, given they wouldn't have to live like any of the marginalized people that would be punished the harshest under such a reign. I actually gave Bernie a lil' money in the first few months of that campaign. I was into his Statler and Waldorf in the form of one socialist man at the beginning until he started to sound too colorblind and crotchety. Then I wanted that donation back so I could put it to use in the form of a catfish sandwich.

But thanks to him, too, using his position to bring greater awareness to the student loan crisis, I will never ask for that refund again.

The people who hated Robert Smith's gift also hated the proposals pushed by both Elizabeth Warren and Bernie Sanders.

Like the parrots they are, detractors dismissed the plans as "bailout." I know corporations are considered people now, but the people who would be assisted by this are human beings suffering, not Ford trucks who need to learn how to be Ford tough. This is equitable taxation that happens to alleviate those drowning in debt as a means to counter the fleecing put forth by financial institutions. Considering all of the rich people and their precious corporations that have been bailed out for effectively scamming Black people with subprime mortgages in addition to other unethical measures that have impacted so many, why not help the generations that have faltered under the broken promise of the American Dream? Why is it so difficult to be decent and considerate?

God, I sound like a senatorial candidate. I'm not running for Senate until I'm in my sixties, for the record. I have too much to create and backlogged thotting to make up for. Plus, I want to make sure Mitch McConnell is good and dead by the time I try to shimmy in.

I went on Elizabeth Warren's campaign site to see how much of my lingering debt would be covered by her plan. I immediately thought of all I could do and how much help I could provide if that were removed from my life. However, given the structure of my private loan debt, chances are the main set of loans that have controlled much of me will have been majorly paid off by the time her plan would be passed and enacted— not including whatever miracles, group prayers, protests, calls, emails, and additional noise are needed to push members of Congress to do the right thing.

I don't feel jealousy over the potential of others having their debts paid off even after I pay off mine. Thankfully, I don't live my life by the mantra "it's all about me-me-me, forget about you-you-you." That's some Republican shit.

All I want is for people to not ever have to feel as low as I've felt dealing with this debt. There are so many of us suffering, quietly, or in my case, not so quietly anymore.

I'd rather people be relieved of the stresses that come with their loans. I want folks to have the freedom to imagine a different experience. To invest in themselves. To help take care of their families. To be able to buy a house and afford the home owner's association costs. To take breaks, vacations, and not tackle work that is beneath them because the thought is outweighed by the reality that falling too far behind on payments will bury their futures. To feel a specific kind of freedom that can only arrive with that problem off their backs. No one should have to turn to a billionaire or game show host to attain this. If anything, treat people drowning in student loan debt like those who created the financial crisis of 2007 and 2008. In this case, it might actually benefit those who need help most.

Of those running for president in 2020, the two millennial candidates, Eric Swalwell (who would eventually be the first candidate to drop out of the race) and Pete Buttigieg, each revealed that they had more than $100,000 in student loan debt (for Buttigieg, most of that debt stems from his husband's student loans). Unless some plan to forgive those debts happens, one day soon there will be for the first time a president who, while in office, will be paying back their student loans from the White House. I wonder, will the bill collectors bug them there? I lean yes.

There is a difference of opinion over whether everyone deserves debt forgiveness. Critics of Sanders's plan argue it would benefit the wealthy more than it will the working class. The top 25 percent of households in the income distribution hold almost half of all student loan debt, according to the Urban Institute, a Washington, D.C.–based think tank. By contrast, the bottom 25 percent hold only about 12 percent. Have a cage match to settle the dispute, but make it quick so debts can be canceled.

This crisis will only worsen with time if major changes aren't enacted. If it's not President Warren or President Sanders ushering the shift in, someone ought to repurpose one of their plans. I don't care. Get it done. Help people. Fix this broken system. Alleviate a looming catastrophe that will impact everyone else. Help us honestly afford avocado toast.

GET US ALL OUT OF THE GHETTO, WHEW CHILE!

I DON'T WANT TO DIE POOR

"**Y**ou know what you need to do?"

My uncle Terry was here and had apparently gone into career counseling since I last saw him.

"You need to stop writing that bullshit on the internet and go write movies like that . . . what's the dumb nigga's name?"

"What nigga, Uncle Terry?"

There are so many dumb niggas out here.

"You know the one. Had all those movies in the eighties. That dumb nigga!"

I was considering texting my friend Amber that ought to be working for the deep state because if you told her "That Dumb Nigga," she would manage to locate the last thing he ordered from Shake Shack if you gave her enough time. I instead waited and allowed my uncle to gather his thoughts for what was now the big reveal.

"Spike Lee! That nigga. You need to go do shit like that."

I thought everyone loved *School Daze*, but apparently not.

But if you are reading this, Tisha Campbell, you did what needed to be done on "Be Alone Tonight."

To be fair to Uncle Terry, this was not bad professional advice. I would love to know how he suddenly had a keener sense about my line of work. Maybe he was watching the *Breakfast Club* interviews or something. I doubt he was reading any of "that bullshit on the internet" that I write. But again, he had a point—no shade to Spike Lee, whose work I have enjoyed and who I wouldn't call a "dumb nigga," though I might politely decline to discuss *Chi-Raq*.

I cannot keep up with the insatiable need for content the internet requires. Well, I can, but I don't think it's healthy to continue for that much longer. I care less and less about most of what manages to rile up the too easily wound up. Most of these publications do not know how to make money, so it doesn't matter what you're writing anyway because the site might not make it for much longer.

So many of them are about to go under, and as someone who had to live through one media bubble bursting, I'm already seeing familiar signs of another one looming. The rush to sell a title before it's too late. The urgent move to consolidate resources without either entity fixing the fundamental problem (realizing you cannot give away free content on the internet for twenty-plus years and expect internet users to automatically start paying for content online). And this country elected a kleptocratic aspiring fascist as president that's bolstered by a political party solely invested in the fleecing of the country's resources on behalf of its astronomically wealthy donors.

Count me out.

But even if everything went swimmingly in media for the foreseeable future—hardy har—television and film writing certainly pay much better than journalism and publishing. Either way, my uncle went from bugging me to burn him DVDs of downloaded movies to seeing me as someone with the ability to make one. What a journey we've been on together. At first, it was "Fuck you do for work? Get a real job, nigga!" and now we have blossomed to "Oh, I saw that nigga on TV. Something's coming."

Uncle Terry's surprisingly sound unsolicited advice then shifted to words of encouragement.

"I always believed in you," he added. "I'm proud of you."

Words of encouragement, that is, driven by a motive.

"You know you gon' take care of your uncle, right?"

Ahh, there we are. It all makes sense now. This man is hilarious.

My dad then promptly snatched the phone away and said of his brother, "That nigga got brain damage, Mike."

Maybe, but when I told my mom, she laughed.

"He meant it, too."

He absolutely meant it. I have two friends back home with the same expectation. I almost feel sorry for taking so long to get out of the hole I've dug myself into. They had plans; I hate being late, even if it always takes me just a little longer to get to wherever I'm supposed to be.

As far as he goes, I'm not taking care of that man, but I will hand him some cash every now and again and a bottle of Paul Masson on a very special future Christmas. Nah, I can do Crown Peach. That's family, distant or not.

I never got the chance to ask him what Spike Lee did to offend him, but White Lee and Tyler Perry may differ in terms of skill set, each share the trait of arguably being heavy-handed in terms of the messaging they want to deliver to their audiences. You want people to understand where you are going from. You want people to take away certain lessons from your story. Yet, while I don't want to don a gray wig or make a weird, ahistorical argument that's going to piss off The Blacks of Twitter in order to do so, I want so desperately to follow that example and nudge the direction of the takeaways from what I've laid bare in this space.

I feel so anxious and concerned about what you—the reader—will take from this. I am not concerned with being canceled. I am not fretting about being taken down. What I do worry about, however, is not being whiny, self-indulgent, or self-pitying, or forging excuses. But there is a shame that comes with not having enough money. We still live in a culture that demonizes people for not having money, like there's something wrong with them. I have carried so much shame with me for so long. I have never wanted to talk about it.

It's easier to write about one's troubles getting to suck dick than it is to reveal how deeply you've questioned whether or not you are sucking at life, or just the mere fear that you are.

I hope I have explained my own bouts with that shame convincingly.

It's just that I have read so many stories about people that have conquered their student loans that only stoke spite from me. If you are to believe what you read, massive debt is not as insurmountable as it sounds. All it requires is discipline, sacrifice, and sheer will.

Stories about how someone paid off $70,000 in loans in nine months. Another one that paid off nearly $30,000 in loans in three years in spite of making $30,000 a year. There's someone else who paid off $87,000 in two and a half years. And a couple that managed to pay off $200,000 in combined loans in nineteen months. I've even read about a guy that took care of his $47,000 in loans in a single year.

They sound like superheroes in the headlines. Their journeys are depicted as both miraculous and attainable—if you just put your all into it. You can will away it all!

I'm supposed to be inspired by their stories. They're supposed to make me believe I can pay it all off faster than I know if I really, really try a little harder. Then you read how they managed to achieve this feat. Mind-shattering tactics such as having a high-earning job that allowed them to make substantial payments toward both the interest and principle of the debt; applying whatever monetary gifts they receive toward their loans; using their bonuses to pay down their debt; make more money.

If I could find a time machine and go back to April 12, 1984, I would whisper the big lotto numbers to my mom right after the umbilical cord was cut from around my neck so that she could be rich and make my life a lot easier. If not that, I could at least return to high school and tell myself to become a lawyer who eventually becomes an anchor that argues with people on prime time like Chris Cuomo. Yes, I will get right on that.

The other methods you read in the stories are no less discontenting.

It's one thing to ask people to go cordless or consider a gymless life, but should we be giving people platforms to share how they paid off their loans by forgoing health insurance, owning a car, having a place of their own? Why are we highlighting people as success stories who felt compelled to stunt their lives to this severity? I'm sure the financial institutions who buy ads around these stories are satisfied, but it comes across as propaganda for lenders. As for the participants, they have every reason to be proud of themselves, but there is no surefire way to pay off massive student loan debt, and to exploit anecdotes in this manner is misguided for all parties involved.

It's never made sense to me. But these stories keep getting presented year after year. On TV and in print and across the internet.

Those people do not need to be mythologized; they need to be listed as more examples of how a corrupt system has soiled the lives of so many. I always want to turn into a Teresa Giudice table-flipping GIF whenever I see these fables pimped out into the zeitgeist. And it's not lost on me how more often than not, when I read these types of stories, the subjects are all white. That does not absolve them of strife, but it majorly provides certain degrees of privilege and access that others reading won't ever have. It's so devoid of reality.

I've gone without everything I've been encouraged to go without. I've done numerous side hustles. I've done every type of writing imaginable—some people simply never knew it. I never understood why Hannah on *Girls* was complaining about advertorial writing—which is basically you writing ad copy. It pays well, and well enough for a person to get their opinions out there for much less, to satisfy their creative urges. I've also done plenty of non-writing and non-media-related jobs—side hustles to my writing and media side hustles. I've done everything I can think of to try and stay afloat and on top of my loans.

I still owe like shit.

I wouldn't say I have a plan to pay off my student loans, but I have an idea of how it's going to go.

Of the low-six figure debt I graduated with, much of it was tied to a consolidation of several loans taken out from one lender per semester that amounted to about $80,000 in debt. I was placed on a twelve-year plan that I had no means of changing. That twelve-year plan is nearly finished. Unfortunately, the rest of that debt—the small private loan and the government loans issued—has ballooned due to interest after several instances of deferment and forbearance. As much as I tried to pay all of them at once, the private loans alone were often too much to tackle. That minimum debt is now substantially more than what it was. So, while that private loan will be paid off in 2021 or 2022 if I'm only paying the minimum, I now owe tens of thousands on the originally low loans.

I may be able to pay them off sooner. I might sell more books. Working in television may go well for me. Someone could pay for my studio time, I could drop bars, and I could pay my loans off and those of my kin (immediate) with the tour sales and #influencer money I plan to scam if I get even a .10 of a hit. Ironically, speaking to college students is the most probable means of me getting out of student loan debt faster.

If none of these options pans out, I will explore other avenues.

I will try to meet a billionaire. I won't be obvious and go to a graduation ceremony anytime soon. I'll think of some other place billionaires hang out. Where is the billionaire let out? I'll go there the second I am sent the location.

I'll start playing lotto regularly. It's no less a gamble than the one I am paying off now. Scratch-offs are fun and make for great birthday gifts in select circles.

I've been told that in order to really, really get ahead, one needs a magic white man to help set you on the right path. Are they supposed to be lying around somewhere just waiting to become the inspiration behind some film that makes white people happy enough that it wins Best Picture at the Academy Awards? Or is this the reality show I should have been pitching all this time? Never mind. I never asked follow-up questions.

Maybe I can go work in tech. I have a few friends who left their fields to go work where the money is. I don't have a lust for wealth, but it would be nice to lead a life no longer dictated by debt. I do not want to die poor, but if all else fails, I'll make sure to get life insurance so that in the event of my untimely death, I won't have to deal with letters going to my tombstone. I suspect Discover Student Loans, my arch nemesis, would find a way to contact me on the hour every hour even in my death. I'd rather be safe than sorry.

Somehow, some way, it will get done. I have to believe that. It's not like I have much of a choice not to believe that. They want the money I owe them in full regardless of whether or not I am physically present to pay it.

But I really, really want to pay them off sooner rather than later. I do not want to be one of those old people paying off their student loans in their seventies. According to the Consumer Financial Protection Bureau, of the more than $1.6 trillion owed in student loan debt, more than 3 million over sixty are paying off $86 billion of that figure. So they are working or having their Social Security benefits garnished. Granted, I doubt we will have Social Security by the time I'm old enough to receive benefits, but that is terrifying.

Your elder years are supposed to be spent in white linen dancing to Charlie Wilson on the Tom Joyner Cruise. I don't want to be seventy-six and unable to go see Cardi B on the boat because I have to go to Walmart in order to change the charger on the robot that manages the distribution center. I read one older person say of their debts, "This will follow me to the grave."

There are older people who find work to keep busy and those who have no choice. Some of those older people working are paying off the loans of their children and grandchildren. I will not do that to my mother. She is retired. She will stay that way.

I'll humble myself as many times as need be to get past this. I'm almost there, but I've always understood how fragile my situation has been. If not for better off friends helping me pay my rent after I stubbornly rebuffed their offerings multiple times, I might not have been able to swing an actual book tour. And if not for being given a hotel gift card from an executive, I might not have made a bookstore stop in a city where I not only got to promote my book, but got to meet with people who can change my life.

Above all, if not for my mom, who doesn't even understand my choices but supports me, there are times in my life where I might not have been able to eat. And this is working day after day for as many people who will have me work in multiple capacities.

So many of the stories about overcoming debt are singular, but there is always the help of others in the backdrop. I hope I have made that clear.

One of my very first published pieces was an essay entitled "Is College Worth It?" Barely out of college, I was already openly weighing my choices: "When I returned home to Texas for a while, several people who had criticized my college ambitions welcomed me back with 'I told you so.' So what do I say now, when people ask me if it was all worth it? My answer is still, 'yes.' College provided opportunities I couldn't have gotten elsewhere. My only regret is that I didn't think of a better way to pay for them."

I have told myself this, but I probably would have skipped

college if I could have, or at least, dropped out midway though. Actually, it doesn't matter. That's been my problem this whole time: I wouldn't stop looking back.

I hope I have made plain how burdensome it can be constantly looking back.

I spent more than a decade letting my loans have a much greater hold on me than I ever should have allowed. The debt was going to be there, but I didn't have to let it drive so much of my thinking. I did not have to convince myself that I did not deserve a certain type of life because I believed that I deserved more than I was told I could have.

I denied myself significant breaks from work, much less real vacations. I have denied myself all sorts of things in the name of fiscal responsibility, or more aptly, not ever defaulting. I sacrificed a lot to stay on top and found myself letting years of my life go by that could have been more favorable to me if I didn't prioritize the interests of my lenders who had no concern over my well-being or over those of my own. And then I punished myself in other ways. I was a person already with demons who piled on myself for having ambition. If I could take a lot of that time back, I would.

I can't, but I hope that I've been convincing enough for others not to ever let themselves stay so stubbornly low.

When my loans are paid off and there are calls for a testimony, I hope I'm as honest as I tried to be here. It's not the preferred route, but it's a more realistic way of how people are living.

I hate those narratives about millennials almost as much as the student loan slayer stories. Year after year we get accused of killing off things.

I've read that we killed porn. I hope you know that I have

done my part to make a contribution. But there is a lengthy and ever-expanding list of things we've purportedly killed.

CREDIT CARDS: LIKE WE NEED MORE DEBT IN OUR LIVES.

MARRIAGE: WHO WANTS TO COMBINE DEBT? LATER IS GREATER. WEDDINGS ARE EXPENSIVE AS HELL.

DIVORCE: IT SOUNDS ALMOST AS EXPENSIVE AS THE WEDDING, SO MIGHT AS WELL CONTINUE SPLITTING THE BILLS.

AMERICAN CHEESE: EWW.

BREAKFAST CEREAL: TOO MUCH SUGAR, AND NO ONE CAN AFFORD TO HAVE DIABETES WITH THIS HEALTH INSURANCE MARKET.

EXORCISMS: THE CATHOLIC CHURCH NEEDS TO TEND TO ITS LIVING DEMONS THAT INAPPROPRIATELY TOUCH CHILDREN.

PRINT MEDIA: BITCH, THAT'S NOT OUR FAULT. AND IT'S NOT OUR FAULT EITHER THAT ONLY TWO COMPANIES CONTROL MOST OF ONLINE ADVERTISING.

GOLF: BORING, AND TIGER WOODS WAS NEVER MOTIVATING ENOUGH, BUT GOOD FOR HIM.

BEER: WINE IS A MORE SOPHISTICATED WAY OF BEING DRUNK, AND HARD LIQUOR IS A MORE FUN WAY OF DRINKING; STOP TRYING TO SQUASH EVOLUTION AND TASTE.

CHAIN RESTAURANTS: APPLEBEE'S NEEDS TO BE HELD ACCOUNTABLE FOR ITS OWN ACTIONS.

SOAP BARS: VINTAGE, BUT LESS CHIC THAN SQUEEZING LIQUID SOAP OUT OF AN ELABORATE DISPENSER.

THE BUSINESS SUIT: MIND YOUR BUSINESS.

LUNCH: THEY'RE PROBABLY WORKING THROUGH LUNCH 'CAUSE MASSA GOT THEM WORKING.

MIDDLE CHILDREN: AS A MIDDLE CHILD, THIS HURTS, BUT CHILDREN ARE EXPENSIVE.

CRUISES: YO, PEOPLE DIE ON BOATS.

THE CANADIAN TOURISM INDUSTRY: THIS CAN'T BE TRUE; THEY HAVE LEGAL WEED AND DRAKE.

RUNNING: I'VE RUN FROM ENOUGH BULLETS IN MY LIFETIME.

MOTORCYCLES: I KNOW SOME PEOPLE TOOK THE ENDING OF *SONS OF ANARCHY* HARD, BUT THEY DID GET THE *MAYANS M.C.* SPINOFF.

THE MOVIES: STOP REBOOTING EVERYTHING—INCLUDING REBOOTING FILMS THAT HAVE ALREADY BEEN REBOOTED BEFORE.

MAYONNAISE: NOT MY TYPE.

CANNED TUNA: NOT MY MINISTRY EITHER.

GAMBLING: WE'VE ALREADY DONE THAT WITH OUR STUDENT LOANS—IT HASN'T WORKED OUT AS WELL AS WE'D LIKE.

DIAMONDS: DROP DEAD.

BRUNCH: BY RUIN, YOU MEAN DAY DRINK OUR SORROWS AWAY TO NUMB THE PAIN? YOU'RE WELCOME, AREA BUSINESSES.

NAPKINS: CLEAN CLOTHS ARE BETTER THAN WASTING PAPER?

GROCERY STORES: IT'S NOT OUR FAULT SOME OF THESE STORES CAN'T KEEP UP WITH TRADER JOE'S, THEIR SISTER IN FOOD SALES, ALDI, OR AMAZON LOWERING PRICES AT WHOLE FOODS.

HOTELS: WHO TOLD THEM TO OVERCHARGE FOR SO LONG?

MALLS: THE AMOUNT OF RETAIL SPACE IN THE UNITED STATES HAS AL- WAYS OUTWEIGHED THAT OF OTHER COUNTRIES.

GYMS: NOT ACCORDING TO MY INSTAGRAM.

PATRIOTISM: SEE TREATMENT OF COLIN KAEPERNICK COMPARED TO THE 45TH PRESIDENT OF THE UNITED STATES OF AMERICA.

THE OLYMPICS: TAPE DELAYS JUST DON'T WORK IN THE INTERNET AGE, LOVES.

HOME OWNERSHIP: MY APOLOGIES FOR NOT BEING ABLE TO COMPETE WITH THE ULTRA-RICH. AND Y'ALL DON'T THINK HOMES OWNED BY BLACK PEOPLE IN BLACK NEIGHBORHOODS ARE WORTH MUCH ANYWAY. I HEARD HOME OWNERSHIP ASSOCIATION FEES ARE HIGH, BY THE WAY.

HOME IMPROVEMENT STORES: THAT'S MY LANDLORD'S PROBLEM.

DEPARTMENT STORES: MACY'S SHOULD HAVE EXTENDED THEIR ONE-DAY SALE FROM BEGINNING TO END, 365 DAYS OF THE YEAR, TO COMPETE WITH FASHION NOVA, FOREVER 21, ASOS, H&M, AND WHEREVER ELSE THOT GEAR FOR MEN AND WOMEN IS SOLD.

SEX: MILLENNIALS ARE FUCKING; THEY MAY JUST CRY LATER WHEN THEY'RE ALONE.

BANKS: LIKE MOST OF US COULD GIVE A FUCK IF THEY CRUMBLE.

THE AMERICAN DREAM: WE CAN FIGHT.

Meanwhile, we're drowning in debt, void of meaning, and the Earth is dying.

In a 2018 report released by economists at the Federal Reserve, they found "Millennials do not appear to have preferences for consumption that differ significantly from those of earlier generations." The problem was that "Millennials are less well off than members of earlier generations when they were young, with lower earnings, fewer assets, and less wealth."

Not to start an intergenerational beef, but I've long found it grating to read piece after piece lamenting millennials ruining everything without acknowledging that baby boomers are directly responsible for many of the challenges faced by Generation X and millennials. I hope that I have offered a narrative that speaks to that, free from the caricatures we've been fed from the minds of the grouchy and deluded. I hope millennials feel heard about entering a job market when employment opportunities were few and far between—resulting in many of us being stuck on lower-paying career trajectories. I hope you can see I share the frustration of being expected to keep up with all that's expected of us—adults—without the wages to do it. I hope I've made the struggles stemming from this palpable.

And while I'm not one to give financial advice, I don't know how many of those experts sleep at night. Giving up an overpriced cup of coffee is not the key to building foundational wealth. And telling people to pay off their loans on time does not constitute advice. I can repeat some of their obvious tips on student loans, but it will ring hollow and probably prove redundant. I can say to those in college to enjoy your forbearance while you can and make as much money as possible. But don't they already know that, too?

I do have some practical tips that I hope will register well.

I'm not encouraging anyone to spend what they don't have, but know that skipping out on treats for yourself is not going to make your life remarkably better in the way debt forgiveness and higher wages would. No, you should not intentionally annihilate your credit score by skipping out on your obligations—although quite a few of you already are, for reasons now more understandable—but please don't go to the extremities some of us have gone to in what may sound good online but might be for naught when practiced individually. Allow yourself enjoyment more often than not. And try to give yourself credit for the accomplishments you achieve, no matter how big or small.

I know that I am now venturing toward Black elder of a Tyler Perry production, ready to instill wisdom in the wayward youth status with this nugget—heavy-handed as hell in administering the "lesson"—but here goes: Learn to forgive yourself. You graduated with debt and that had you stepping out into the world without a clean slate. That plus the influences around you may now have caused you to think less of yourself.

Have your low moments, but please don't stew in them the way your OGs have. Remember you only did what you thought was best at the time. You didn't know better. You thought it would be better after you got out. The system, as it is designed now, is set up for your failure. You don't want to sound like one of those sad statistics, but you are in the same boat. Forgive yourself for all of that. Do what you can and pay what you can and allow yourself a little joy in the meanwhile. How I learned to stop denying myself pleasure in the physical sense for my sexuality, but not in my head about debt, is my own cross to bear, but while you cannot forgive Kanye West or Mean Mary of Mary Mary for vocalizing support of Donald Trump, you can forgive yourself for this and whatever failures you've experienced that are real, and those merely perceived.

The sooner you do that—truly do it rather than bullshitting yourself about that fact the way I used to—the lighter you will feel. If I can only get readers to pull one ideal from my attempts with this body of work, I hope it's at least that.

ACKNOWLEDGMENTS

I would like to begin this portion of the book as if I just won Best R&B/Soul album at the Soul Train Music Awards. To that end, first and foremost, I would like to thank the creator for whom all things are possible. (Note that I did not identify the creator as an incredibly old but remarkably fit white man with a fresh sew-in weave. I'm still not *saved*, but I'm not Black Bill Maher either, beloveds.)

Secondly, I would like to thank my parents who, like The Lord, have made all things possible for me. I remain forever grateful to them as well as siblings, my big sister Nicole and little brother Marcus, my stunning nieces Alexis and Alyssa, and the rest of my family.

I would like to thank my agent, Jim McCarthy at Dystel, Goderich & Bourret, for helping me get to the finish line once more. Thank you to my dear editor, Rakesh Satyal, for once again believing in the stories I wanted to share with the world. Writing this book was more challenging than I envisioned, so I appreciate you both for alleviating my worries at the end.

Thank you to my other agent, Jason Richman at UTA, and my manager, Jermaine Johnson at 3 Arts, for helping me with the next stages of my career. In other words, for getting me the type of work that will finally put down the last of my student-loan debt.

Thank you, a thousand times, to my folk: Kimberly, dré, Jeanne, Janet, Jason, Devon, Jessica, Sadé, Corey, Lauren, Alba, Melanie, Luis, Steven, Marc, Murdoc, Nikki, Darnell, Bassey, Nakea, Alex, Robert, Samantha, Brandon, Nakisha, Maiya, Doreen, Rhonda, Sylvia, Melissa, Richie, Kierna, Sarah, Rembert, Mimi, Damien, Jai, Gina, Zach, Dara, Lena, Denene, Desus, Mero, and Bevy. To my other friends, you can cuss me smooth out later. I'll still love you and be most grateful, though. Thank you in particular to Richelle Carey, Bomani Jones, Kirk Moore, and Tiffany Williams.

Sweet, sweet Mark: rest well. You, too, Uncle Terry. I'm still so sorry, but I love and miss you both.

As always, I love you, Houston. Shout out to Hiram Clarke. And thank you, Beyoncé. Just because.

Lastly, a huge thanks to each one of you who has supported *I Can't Date Jesus*, and now, *I Don't Want To Die Poor*. Thank you for helping me prove to myself that what I have to say and the ways in which I choose to say it have value. It means the world.

More to come.

ABOUT THE AUTHOR

M ichael Arceneaux is the *New York Times* bestselling author of *I Can't Date Jesus: Love, Sex, Family, Race, and Other Reasons I've Put My Faith in Beyoncé*. He has written for the *New York Times*, the *Washington Post*, *Essence*, *Esquire*, *Ebony*, *Elle*, *Rolling Stone*, and many, many other publications on and off Al Gore's internet. He's ran his mouth on MSNBC, NPR, VH1, Viceland, Comedy Central, SiriusXM, and elsewhere. He really, really can't wait to pay off his student loans.